Tune-In Heaven

Blessings, Protection and Joy

First Edition

Leonard Zagurskie, Jr.

~

Tune-In Heaven, Blessings, Protection & Joy

By Leonard Zagurskie, Jr.

Published by Leonard Zagurskie, Jr.

Cover Design and Drawings by Leonard Zagurskie, Jr.

Editing Assist by Regina Aflleje Zagurskie

Contents

Tune-In Heaven
Introduction

There is a Higher Power. There are fixed precepts that shape
our lives in this world and in the next. If you know them then
you can make choices so that you receive the blessings, the
Lord's Joy, Protection and Prosperity or otherwise your life
appears fortuitous and you repeat cycles and behaviors. Are
you interested in making positive changes in life and
receiving the Blessings and the Protection of God Almighty,
and entering into the Joy of the Lord, the Higher Power, the
Creator God, the Protector, the Holy One, the Redeemer?
Then to Tune-In Heaven, you need to know these seven
precepts so you can be aware when these choices are
presented:

➢ Truth. You cannot benefit from false doctrine. You can
only benefit from knowing the truth and acting upon the
truth. For example, if you have a phony bus schedule then
sometimes you catch a bus and other times a bus never
comes. Just like catching a bus your life appears
fortuitous. Truth is worthy even so much more worthy
than a true bus schedule. Truth is wholly worthy.

➢ The Higher Power, Creator God of the Universe, the
Good Heavenly Father, the Redeemer, gave you the
power to choose.

➢ If you complain then there is where you get stuck.
Delight and commit one's way to the Lord. Obey His
Commandments. Tune-In Blessings, Prosperity and Joy!

➢ What you hold in your heart then that is what you attract. The God of the Universe, the Higher Power, the Good Heavenly Father that loves you and desires to give you the good desires of your heart is wholly worthy. And, you will get the desires of your heart!

➢ The only behavior you can change is your own behavior. Trying to change someone else's behavior is manipulation also it is witchcraft.

➢ When evil is intended, the Higher Power, the God of the universe, the Good Heavenly Father, the Holy One, the Redeemer, Who knows and loves His own and they know Him, the Protector thwarts the evil and brings about justice and makes it for good to be achieved.

Vengeance is the Lords. When evil is intended against you He redirects it back to sender and utterly destroys the evil or the Lord means it for good, many are saved and He lets you enter into His Joy and gives you the good desires of your heart and is wholly worthy.

➢ You can have a personal relationship with the Higher Power, the Holy One, the God of the Universe, the Good Heavenly Father, the Creator God, the Redeemer.

The Lord is accessible from any place at any time. He is now reaching out to you as the prophet Isaiah declares: "God's arms are stretched out still." You can picture Jesus on the cross with His outstretched arms, and now His arms are stretched out to us to enter into His Joy and receive His Blessings, Prosperity and Protection.

And now imagine knowing these precepts that shape our lives in this world and in the next, accordingly you can choose the Lord's Blessings, Joy, Protection and Prosperity.

As many of you already know there absolutely is a Higher Power, the Holy One, the Holy Spirit, who is the Creator of the Universe, the Redeemer. He wants to give you the good desires of your heart. He is the Good Heavenly Father.

You are Tuning Into Heaven as you learn these Biblical precepts. Also you will more easily recognize the Lord in the Scriptures the closer you get to know the Lord. He reveals himself more to you as the more you get to know His precepts. And the closer you get to the Lord the more Blessings you will receive right here, right now, today and the Joy of the Lord that surpasses all understanding.

Just as one recognizes someone who will become a friend and then becomes a friend so it is with the Higher Spirit, the Holy One, the Redeemer, the Creator God of the Universe who is the Good Heavenly Father. When you read any one of the four Gospels of the New Testament you begin to recognize the Lord by His Words.

Jesus is the good shepherd. He knows His sheep and they know Him. The Gospel of John:

▶ 14. I am the good shepherd, and know my sheep, and am known of mine.
15. As the Father knoweth me, even so know I the Father: and I lay down my life for the sheep.
John 10: 14-15

Wait you may say: You are quoting Bible verses. I the Reader am not sure about the Bible.

Answer: I the Author promise: upcoming in *Chapter 7*, *You Can Trust the Bible*, later in this book, covers with specificity the authenticity of the Bible as the inspired word of the Lord. The Bible is more trust worthier than any other writing. There is as much or more evidence to the authenticity of the Bible than any other historical document. Therefore, we rely on the Bible in our studies and our lives!

The Bible illustrates real individuals, not storybook characters, yes, real individuals with actual personal relationships with the Higher Power, the God of the Universe, the Holy One, the Redeemer who experienced the Protection, the Blessings and Joy of the Lord. The details of their struggles and heartfelt emotions are experienced as you read and learn these precepts when you read the Bible. Read the Bible the awesome word of the Lord.

The focus of "Tuning in Heaven" is on identifying and outlining these precepts. With knowing, choosing and applying these precepts you too can enter into the Blessings, the Prosperity, the Joy and the Protection of the Higher Power, the Higher Spirit, the Holy One, the Lord, the Creator God, God Almighty, the Good Heavenly Father, the Redeemer.

Keep reading Tune-In Heaven, become aware and grow conscious of these life-changing precepts! I am going to go through this fast and it is a lot of material so hold on. Stay with it. You will not be disappointed. You may want to reflect after you read some of the book then come back and read further or you may want to speed read or what I call rifle read through some of the book reading passages that catch your eye. Then return for an in-depth read.

When you are informed for the very first time with any precept in this book it is truly an amazing, real eye opener - a life changer, because these principles are absolutely real and utterly life transforming. As you will learn!

You too can learn these precepts, apply them and Tune-In Heaven.

As you Tune-In Heaven and become more aware of the Higher Spirit, the Creator God of the Universe, the Holy One, the Lord, the Redeemer you experience the Blessings and the Protection of the Lord and enter into the Joy, of God Almighty.

- - - - - - - --

WHAT YOU NEED TO KNOW ABOUT BIBLICAL QUOTED SCRIPTURES AND REFERENCES IN THIS BOOK:

All Biblical quoted scriptures and references in this book are from the King James Version (KJV) of the Bible.

KJV scriptures are presented in the KJV format with no changes to the outdated wording and spelling.

The symbol: ▶ indicates that scripture from the KJV of the Bible follows.

Immediately before quoted scripture "Notes" provide helpful definitions of words used in the upcoming scripture.

After the quoted KJV scripture then on the next line is stated the Bible book, chapter and verse.

CHAPTER 1

~

No Complaining

The first precept you must learn is to stop complaining!
No matter what picture you have in your mind of Heaven,
it does not include complaining. Can you imagine Apostle
Paul, Apostle Peter or anyone complaining about anything in
Heaven, for example, that the golden streets are somewhat
less than spectacular? Of course not! You cannot "Tune Into"
the Blessings of the Lord if you complain - then there is
where you get stuck. Read on to learn how this precept
works.

In the old days they used the word "murmuring" which
means complaining. When reading Bible verses about
complaining substitute complaining for murmuring:

Note: the destroyer is Satan.

▶ Neither murmur ye, as some of them also murmured, and
were destroyed of the destroyer.

1 Corinthians 10:10

▶ Do all things without murmurings and disputings,

Philippians 2:14

▶ In every thing give thanks: for this is the will of God in
Christ Jesus concerning you.

1 Thessalonians 5:18

▶ Let no corrupt communication proceed out of your mouth, but that, which is good to the use of edifying, that it may minister grace unto the hearers.

Ephesians 4:29

▶ Not that I speak in respect of want: for I have learned, in whatsoever state I am, therewith to be content.

Philippians 4:11

▶ A merry heart doeth good like a medicine: but a broken spirit drieth the bones.

Proverbs 17:22

OK you may say, I got it: The Bible says not to complain. But how does this relate to "Tuning into Heaven" and receiving the Blessings of the Higher Power?

Answer: First, the Blessings come from the Lord, God Almighty, the Protector, the Higher Power the Creator God, the Good Heavenly Father, the Holy One, the Redeemer. He is the source of the Blessings:

▶ The blessing of the LORD, it maketh rich, and he addeth no sorrow with it.

Proverbs 10:22

▶ Thus saith the LORD, thy Redeemer, the Holy One of Israel; I am the LORD thy God which teacheth thee to profit, which leadeth thee by the way that thou shouldest go.

Isaiah 48:17

▶ But thou shalt remember the LORD thy God: for it is he that giveth thee power to get wealth, that he may establish his covenant which he sware unto thy fathers, as it is this day.

Deuteronomy 8:18

How to Love the Lord:

So if the Blessings come from the Higher Power, God
Almighty, the Creator God, the Good Heavenly Father,
the Holy One, the Redeemer, then how does one "Tune Into"
these Blessings? The answer is you must love the Lord,
which means to follow His Commandments:

▶ If you love me, keep my commands.

John 14:15

▶ That I may cause those that love me to inherit substance;
and I will fill their treasures.

Proverbs 8:21

▶ Jesus answered and said unto him, If a man love me, he
will keep my words: and my Father will love him, and we
will come unto him, and make our abode with him.

John 14: 23

How to Love One Another:

Loving the Lord is keeping His Commandments therefore love
requires action. Love is what one does. Love is behavior. Love
is how one treats another. Love is much more than just saying
sweet nothings, empty words and excess dramatics. Love is
action: Treating another one with respect, kindly and considerate
of feelings - that is love. Love is expressed and measured by
how one has treated another and what one has done for another.
It is not just saying it: It is doing it!

You do for someone things that they like and desire. Not
what you like and enjoy. You need to be observant as to what
they enjoy. Then that is what you do.

Note: Take caution. Being taken advantage of is not love.
It is being beguiled, swindled and cheated.

Loving the Lord and Receiving His Blessings:

So then "loving the Lord," which is keeping His commandments, ensures us of His blessings. Deuteronomy 28: 1-14 fully explains and describes the Lord's Blessings:

The Lord's Blessings:

▶ 1. And it shall come to pass, if thou shalt hearken diligently unto the voice of the LORD thy God, to observe and to do all his commandments which I command thee this day, that the LORD thy God will set thee on high above all nations of the earth:

2. And all these blessings shall come on thee, and overtake thee, if thou shalt hearken unto the voice of the LORD thy God.

3. Blessed shalt thou be in the city, and blessed shalt thou be in the field.

4. Blessed shall be the fruit of thy body, and the fruit of thy ground, and the fruit of thy cattle, the increase of thy kine, and the flocks of thy sheep.

5. Blessed shall be thy basket and thy store.

6. Blessed shalt thou be when thou comest in, and blesse shalt thou be when thou goest out.

7. The LORD shall cause thine enemies that rise up against thee to be smitten before thy face: they shall come out against thee one way, and flee before thee seven ways.

8. The LORD shall command the blessing upon thee in thy storehouses, and in all that thou settest thine hand unto; and he shall bless thee in the land which the LORD thy God giveth thee.

9. The LORD shall establish thee an holy people unto himself, as he hath sworn unto thee, if thou shalt keep the commandments of the LORD thy God, and walk in his ways.

10. And all people of the earth shall see that thou art called by the name of the LORD; and they shall be afraid of thee.

11. And the LORD shall make thee plenteous in goods, in the fruit of thy body, and in the fruit of thy cattle, and in the fruit of thy ground, in the land which the LORD sware unto thy fathers to give thee.

12. The LORD shall open unto thee his good treasure, the heaven to give the rain unto thy land in his season, and to bless all the work of thine hand: and thou shalt lend unto many nations, and thou shalt not borrow.

13. And the LORD shall make thee the head, and not the tail; and thou shalt be above only, and thou shalt not be beneath; if that thou hearken unto the commandments of the LORD thy God, which I command thee this day, to observe and to do them:

14. And thou shalt not go aside from any of the words, which I command thee this day, to the right hand, or to the left, to go after other gods to serve them.

Deuteronomy 28: 1-14

You get blessings when you follow the Lord's Commandments.

So what is the point?

Answer: You get blessings if you follow the Lord's commandments:

The Lord's Ten Commandments are found in the Bible in Exodus 20:2-17 and in Deuteronomy 5:6-21. Other commandments such as "no complaining" are not as well recognized. But profoundly impact the Blessings, the Protection and the Joy.

Why would complaining profoundly impact Blessings?

Answer: Complaining is not obeying the Lord. Not obeying the Lord is sinning. In the Bible, in Deuteronomy 28: 15-45, the curses of disobedience are listed. Clearly the curses are the direct opposite of the blessings. Complaining not only blocks the Blessings but also attracts the Lord's curses!

So then if one complains then there is where one gets stuck. The cycle repeats. Complaining blocks the Blessings and attracts the Lord's curses!

Also the Lord is a fair and just Lord, so He will only hold you accountable for what you know. So you know now and you can no longer use that excuse. It is better that you know. This way you can Tune-In the Blessings, Prosperity and Joy.

As most of the readers know if you ask Jesus to forgive you for your sins He will forgive you for any sin.

The Jurisdiction of the Lord is the Heart.

He knows your heart.
Note: Countenance means face.

▶ But the Lord said unto Samuel, Look not on his countenance, or on the height of his stature; because I have refused him: for the Lord seeth not as man seeth; for man looketh on the outward appearance, but the Lord looketh on the heart.
1 Samuel 16:7

You can personally approach the Lord in prayer and ask to be forgiven and He will forgive you. You can do that right now and He will forgive you. If you desire to reconcile with the Lord, in prayer, call upon the name of the Lord and ask Him for forgiveness. Also, please keep in mind that many folks after asking the Lord for forgiveness then unfortunately the learning ends and the experience fades. Instead you can revitalize your faith, or make it the beginning: Keep learning and knowing God more. Delight and commit one's way to the Lord. Obey His Commandments. Tune-In Heaven.

Righteous Indignation Anger:

God's anger is an extensive fascinating topic. God is angered by sin. Likewise we are angered by sin. In the Bible are examples of the Lord's Holy Anger, referred to as the Lord's Righteous Indignation Anger. Sin such as complaining can kindle the Lord's anger. After the Lord delivered the Hebrews out of the bondage of slavery in Egypt the complaining of some of the Hebrews displeased the Lord and the Lord's fire consumed them:

▶ 1. And when the people complained, it displeased the Lord: and the Lord heard it; and his anger was kindled; and the fire of the Lord burnt among them, and consumed them that were in the uttermost parts of the camp.

2. And the people cried unto Moses; and when Moses prayed unto the Lord, the fire was quenched.
Numbers 11:1-2

The Lord is the champion of strangers (immigrants/aliens), widows and the fatherless children. The Lord warns not to harass, terrorize or cause problems for strangers, widows and the fatherless child, as He will hear their cry, His wrath will wax hot and the Lord will take the offender's life:

▶ 21. Thou shalt neither vex a stranger, nor oppress him: for ye were strangers in the land of Egypt.

22. Ye shall not afflict any widow, or fatherless child.

23. If thou afflict them in any wise, and they cry at all unto me, I will surely hear their cry;

24. And my wrath shall wax hot, and I will kill you with the sword; and your wives shall be widows, and your children fatherless.

Exodus 22: 21-24

As God is angered by sin in a very similar way so are we angered by sin. We are not to take matters into our own hands, except for very limited circumstances such as to save life: We are law and order!

We can tell it like it is and let the truth be known! Truth is wholly worthy. We are not complaining. We are voicing our concerns. We have no joy in sin! Vengeance is the Lords. When evil is intended He thwarts the evil and brings about justice and makes good be achieved.

▶ Be ye angry, and sin not: let not the sun go down upon your wrath:

Ephesians 4:26

Fortunately for us, sinful mankind, the Lord is Abundant in Mercy, Grace and is Slow to Anger:

Note: chide means reprimand.

▶ 8. The Lord is merciful and gracious, slow to anger, and plenteous in mercy.

9. He will not always chide: neither will he keep his anger for ever

10. He hath not dealt with us after our sins; nor rewarded us according to our iniquities.

11. For as the heaven is high above the earth, so great is his mercy toward them that fear him.

12. As far as the east is from the west, so far hath he removed our transgressions from us.

13. Like as a father pitieth his children, so the Lord pitieth them that fear him.

14. For he knoweth our frame; he remembereth that we are dust.

15. As for man, his days are as grass: as a flower of the field, so he flourisheth.

16. For the wind passeth over it, and it is gone; and the place thereof shall know it no more.

17. But the mercy of the Lord is from everlasting to everlasting upon them that fear him, and his righteousness unto children's children;

Psalm 103:8-17

The Lord Loves You and Wants to Give You the Good Desires of your Heart:

The Higher Power, the Creator of the Universe, the Holy One, the Good Heavenly Father, the Redeemer wants to give you the good desires of your heart as Jesus explains:

▶ 7. Ask, and it shall be given you; seek, and ye shall find; knock, and it shall be opened unto you:

8. For every one that asketh receiveth; and he that seeketh findeth; and to him that knocketh it shall be opened.

9. Or what man is there of you, whom if his son ask bread, will he give him a stone?

10. Or if he ask a fish, will he give him a serpent?

11. If ye then, being evil, know how to give good gifts unto your children, how much more shall your Father which is in heaven give good things to them that ask him?
Luke 11:7-11

The Lord loves you and wants to give you the good desires of your heart. But if you complain there is where you get stuck. Think of the parents who gives their child a gift and then the child complains about the gift. How does the parents feel? So how do you think the Lord feels when one complains?

Stop Complaining, Instead Give the Lord Thanks.
Stop complaining. Plainly you will be more content.
Instead give thanks to the Lord as the Bible directs:

► In every thing give thanks: for this is the will of God in Christ Jesus concerning you.
1 Thessalonians 5:18

► And whatsoever ye do in word or deed, [do] all in the name of the Lord Jesus, giving thanks to God and the Father by him.
Colossians 3:17

► Fear thou not; for I [am] with thee: be not dismayed; for I [am] thy God: I will strengthen thee; yea, I will help thee; yea, I will uphold thee with the right hand of my righteousness.
Isaiah 41:10

Thank the Lord right now for getting to know the Higher Power the Creator God, the Good Heavenly Father, the Holy One, the Redeemer, so much better. He is now reaching out to you and now you know Him better.

STOP COMPLAINING so that you receive the Blessings, the Lord's Joy, Protection and Prosperity or otherwise your life appears fortuitous and you repeat cycles and behaviors. Are you interested in making positive changes in life and receiving the Blessings, the Protection of God Almighty?

Tune Into the Lord's Blessings.

HERE ARE YOUR GIFTS

THANK YOU

I HATE IT!

Gift

Gift

Are you pleasing the Lord?

One can receive the Gifts of the Lord with thanks or one can cast away the Gifts of the Lord with complaints

And, are you interested in entering into the Joy of the Lord, the Higher Power the Creator God, the Good Heavenly Father, the Holy One, the Redeemer? Then stop complaining and in everything give thanks!

When one complains then there is where one gets stuck. Complaining blocks the Blessings and attracts the Lord's curses! The cycles repeat.

Become observant so that you can see in other people when they are complaining and how the patterns and cycles continue and how they are stuck there. Also you will see it in yourself. You will catch yourself complaining. So then the next time, catch yourself about to complain, then instead of complaining just thank the Lord. You have many countless reasons to thank the Lord.

If for example you are in a traffic jam, thank the Lord that you already stopped for gas before you ramped onto the expressway.

If you are running out of gas thank the Lord that you have a cell phone and can telephone roadside assistance, and so on and so on.

Everyone knows that there is someone else out there going through a much worse encounter.

And thank the Lord right now for getting to know the Higher Power the Creator God, the Good Heavenly Father, the Holy One, the Redeemer, a great deal better. He is now reaching out to you and now you know Him even better.

I use to complain because every time that I was driving my car and I would come to a highway exit - it was so incredible, it continually reoccurred - a big truck, driving in the traffic would every time be blocking my view of the exit sign of the exit that I needed to take. I would vehemently complain!

CHAPTER 1
No Complaining

So after I understood not to complain but to give thanks, then I gave thanks to the Lord. Therefore, instead the next time that a big truck started blocking the exit, I started to thank the Lord that I had enough time to get over and properly exit and I thanked the Lord for many, many other things as well!

I thanked the Lord instead of complaining and the reoccurring circumstance of the big truck blocking the exit sign stopped!

Yes, it is true. You try it. See it for yourself! Become aware of what you are complaining about. Then exchange whatever you are complaining about with Thanks to the Lord.
Thank you Jesus!

Give the Lord thanks in all things! You will not only become more contented, you will free yourself from being stuck, you will please the Lord and obtain the Blessings and Protection of God Almighty, the Higher Power the Creator God, the Good Heavenly Father, the Holy One, the Redeemer.

Thank you Lord! Thank you Father, Son and Holy Spirit.

GOD GAVE US THE POWER TO CHOOSE

The Higher Power the Creator God, the Good Heavenly Father, the Holy One, the Redeemer, has given us the power to choose from the very beginning.

Ever since the Lord made the Garden of Eden for Adam and Eve, God Almighty desired our lives to be joy. Adam and Eve were empowered with the ability to make a decision – a choice. We have freedom of choice. Always choose joy and choose to do the right thing.

Freedom of Choice: Always Choose Joy and Choose to Do the Right Thing!

Guideline, Steps:

First, you always have one out of three (3) basic choices. Out of the three basic choices: Choose joy.
Next you are presented with two (2) conflicting, opposing and incompatible choices, the Lord or Satan, synonymously good or evil. Always choose the Lord and do the right thing.

Instructions, Explanations:

First: how do I choose Joy out of three (3) basic choices?

Answer: It is easy to make a positive decision to choose joy. The mind receives information (experiences), processes the information (thinking), then you make a decision (choice).

An example of making a positive decision to choose joy out of three (3) choices is presented in the following hypothetical event: A hypothetical person named Joe was just informed that his vehicle was demolished, totaled, completely destroyed, in the parking lot as a result of being slammed into by an out of control huge truck.

While Joe is processing this information let us suppose that Joe's vehicle was fully insured, although one hundred (100) percent financed, but historically unreliable and prior to the slam the vehicle's transmission had spun-out in the parking lot, so then earlier it was in need of a tow to the shop. Now can you see the smile start to appear on Joe's face!
Joe knows that the insurance will completely pay off the vehicle loan, the vehicle will be towed away and Joe will be able to get a replacement vehicle. Joe chooses to be happy.

But wait a minute let us reverse the hypothetical facts. Let us say that the vehicle ran perfect, was historically dependable and that Joe absolutely needed the vehicle to go on a job interview the next morning at eight o'clock. Because Joe's unemployment compensation ended a week ago, he is out of money and he had received an eviction notice, so Joe absolutely needs to gets to that eight o'clock interview.
Can you see that smile getting wiped off of Joe's face?

Joy: Joe has a third choice:
Joy is different than happy. Happy is derived from happenstance. Happenstance is an occurrence by chance: Choice based on happenstance leads to a roller coaster ride of emotions, whereas, Joy is a gift from the Lord. Joy is enduring, unchanging and steadfast. James the brother of Jesus instructs us to consider all trials and tribulations joy.

Note: divers means diverse/various.

Note: temptations also translates as trials.

▶ My brethren, count it all joy when ye fall into divers temptations;
James 1:2

Choosing joy, not complaining, praising and giving thanks to the Lord develops trust in the Lord. Trusting in the Lord gives way to entering into the Joy of the Lord. No better example of Joy and the enduring, steadfast Trust in the Lord than Psalm 30 by King David.

▶ 11. Thou hast turned for me my mourning into dancing: thou hast put off my sackcloth, and girded me with gladness;

12. To the end that my glory may sing praise to thee, and not be silent. O LORD my God, I will give thanks unto thee forever.
Psalm 30: 11-12

Praise you Lord, Praise you Jesus, Thank you Father, Son and Holy Spirit. I choose to thank and praise you Lord. I break out into praising the Lord. Praise the Lord as found in another Psalm by King David:

▶ 1. Praise ye the Lord. Praise God in his sanctuary: praise him in the firmament of his power.

2. Praise him for his mighty acts: praise him according to his excellent greatness.

3. Praise him with the sound of the trumpet: praise him with the psaltery and harp.

4. Praise him with the timbrel and dance: praise him with stringed instruments and organs.

5. Praise him upon the loud cymbals: praise him upon the high sounding cymbals.

6. Let every thing that hath breath praise the Lord. Praise ye the Lord.

Psalm 150: 1-6

CHAPTER 2

~

What you hold in your heart then that is what you attract.

The Higher Power, the Creator God, the Good Heavenly Father, the Holy One, the Redeemer gave you the power to make choices. So then what shapes our decisions to make a specific choice is our beliefs, our desires and also outside influences. The beliefs you hold in your heart shape your decisions regardless of whether you understand these beliefs as fact, supernatural or theory. They shape your decisions if you hold them in your heart. Will they shape your decisions in order to attract the Blessings or the curses?

<u>Freedom of Choice</u>. Choose that which is Good
What you hold in your Heart starts in your Mind.

It is easy to make a decision to choose what is right. The mind receives information (experiences), processes the information (thinking), then you make a decision (choice). Always choose joy and choose what is the right thing to do.

As discussed in Chapter One: Choose the Joy of the Lord, not one of the two modes of happenstance: happiness or unhappiness. Next two (2) choices are the Lord or Satan, synonymous with good or evil. Always choose the Lord and that which is good and do the right thing. And, always do the right thing no matter what! Everybody can be doing the wrong thing. You are required to do the right thing.

Repeating Cycles and Behaviors

When events are occurring rapidly choices can be made out of habit, that is, with only minimal thought.

You need to get control of your decision making process. Here is the trap of repeating cycles and behaviors. You need to focus on events and become aware of habit decisions you are making during events that reoccur.

If, for example you discover that you just made a bad decision: you complained. Be prepared for the next time that type of event occurs to change your response: instead of complaining be prepared to give thanks and to praise the Lord and break the cycle. Then you begin to hold the Joy in your heart and begin to attract the Lord's Blessings.

Now moving on wholeheartedly into the next two (2) choices of choosing the Lord or choosing Satan, the same as good or evil. This is powerful! When you accept or reject the Lord, always remember that rejecting the Lord or the Lord's way is equivalent to choosing Satan and evil and to continue in sin:

The Word of the Lord Convicts: Two (2) Choices.

There absolutely is the Higher Power the Creator God, the Good Heavenly Father, the Holy One, the Redeemer, that actually truly exits! To grasp this precept of "what you hold in your heart then that is what you attract" you must understand that the Word of the Lord "convicts" a person and then you make one of the two choices: either to accept or reject the Lord:

CHAPTER 2
What you hold in your heart
that is what you attract.

The first choice is to accept the Lord and confess your sin and the Lord will redeem you. Absolutely! His jurisdiction is the heart and He desires that everyone to be saved.

When Apostle Peter preached after Pentecost they were "pricked in their heart" and then they repented:

▶ 36. Therefore let all the house of Israel know assuredly, that God hath made the same Jesus, whom ye have crucified, both Lord and Christ.

37. Now when they heard this, they were pricked in their heart, and said unto Peter and to the rest of the apostles, Men and brethren, what shall we do?

38. Then Peter said unto them, Repent, and be baptized every one of you in the name of Jesus Christ for the remission of sins, and ye shall receive the gift of the Holy Ghost.

39. For the promise is unto you, and to your children, and to all that are afar off, even as many as the Lord our God shall call.

40. And with many other words did he testify and exhort, saying, save yourselves from this untoward generation.

41. Then they that gladly received his word were baptized: and the same day there were added unto them about three thousand souls.

Acts 2: 36-41

Again you have one of two choices when the word of the Lord "Convicts" a person. This second choice occurred after Apostle Stephen preached and they were "cut to the heart" they chose the second choice: to reject the Lord and continue in their sin:

▶ 54 When they heard these things, they were cut to the heart, and they gnashed on him with their teeth.

55. But he, being full of the Holy Ghost, looked up steadfastly into heaven, and saw the glory of God, and Jesus standing on the right hand of God,

56. and said, Behold, I see the heavens opened, and the Son of man standing on the right hand of God.

57. Then they cried out with a loud voice, and stopped their ears, and ran upon him with one accord,

58. and cast him out of the city, and stoned him....
Acts 7: 54-58

Choose the Lord. Choose the Lord's way. God gave you the ability to make decisions. Always choose to do the right thing, no matter what everyone else is doing! Choose the right way! You always do the right thing! Run from evil! Commit yourself to the Lord's ways.

Choose as those who listened to Apostle Peter preach the Gospel after Pentecost, who were "pricked in their heart" they repented. Choose to learn these precepts that are found in the Bible and enter into the Blessings, the Joy and the Protection of the Lord, the Good Heavenly Father, the Holy One who is the Higher Spirit who is the Creator of the Universe, the Redeemer.

Be Encouraged:
Be encouraged. Folks who are experiencing this for the first time, realizing that the Lord is truly powerful, able and is God Almighty be encouraged because this is not a hard thing. The same Lord loves us. He is also the Good Heavenly Father desiring for us to enter into His Joy and receive His Blessings. He is a Personal God who is always here for us. Also He is the Redeemer. He personally paid for our sins with His life. Along with His knowledge the Lord promises:

CHAPTER 2
What you hold in your heart
that is what you attract.

▶ The fear of the Lord is the beginning of knowledge: but fools despise wisdom and instruction.

Proverbs 1:7

▶ For my yoke is easy, and my burden is light.

Matthew 11:30

▶ And he said, The things which are impossible with men are possible with God.

Luke 18:27

▶ And Jesus looking upon them saith, with men it is impossible, but not with God: for with God all things are possible.

Mark 10:27

What you hold in your heart then that is what you attract. The Lord will provide you the desires of your heart. The Creator God of the Universe, the Higher Power, the Holy One, the Redeemer that gives the power to choose. It starts in one's mind then moves to the heart. Apostle Paul instructs us to think of good things.

▶ Finally, brethren, whatsoever things are true, whatsoever things are honest, whatsoever things are just, whatsoever things are pure, whatsoever things are lovely, whatsoever things are of good report; if there be any virtue, and if there be any praise, think on these things.

Philippians 4:8

Now you need to reflect on what you hold in your heart. Get right with the Lord. Repent of your sins to Jesus. He will forgive you. Desire the good things. Make an effort to hold the good things in your heart. The Lord helps you overcome.

WARNING: This is private. You do not share what you hold in your heart with others. As Jesus has warned us in the Gospel of Matthew:

Note: Rend means to separate or tear into parts.

▶ Give not that which is holy unto the dogs, neither cast ye your pearls before swine, lest they trample them under their feet, and turn again and rend you.

Matthew 7:6

Not everyone will have encouraging words for the new believer. There are ones who will "rend" the new believer.

Reprobate:

So what you desire in your heart is what the Creator God of the Universe, the Higher Power will give you or better put is that: He allows you to choose. Choose the Lord's way. Or, if you choose to permit your desire to be evil then what do you think you are going to get? Answer: Not the blessings. No way! You will receive evil! Then in continuing to desire evil where can that lead?

Answer: Reprobate

As Paul explains in his letter to the Romans "God gave them over to a reprobate mind"

Note: the word "reprobate" means wicked and worthless.

Note: Convenient means "proper."

▶ And even as they did not like to retain God in their knowledge, God gave them over to a reprobate mind, to do those things which are not convenient;

Romans 1:28

CHAPTER 2
What you hold in your heart
that is what you attract.

Reprobate does not include an apologetic heart that is remorseful and feels sorrowful over sin, as we are all sinners and fall short: Even ashamed to the Lord. The desire of the repentant heart was good not evil. Whereas, a reprobate heart does "not like to retain God in their knowledge."

They were given over to a "reprobate mind" that is a wicked and worthless mind! It is dreadful to think of a person in such a lost state! Abandoned by God!

The Lord allows choice. So what you desire in your heart is what is attracted. If you choose to permit your desire to be evil then you do not the receive blessings. You receive evil! Apostle Paul explains in a letter to Titus:

Apostle Paul began/originated the Church in Crete. He could not stay there at the Church so he established Titus to lead the church congregation in Crete. Afterwards Paul sent a letter to instruct and encourage Titus.

In the letter Paul warns that some folks have knowledge of the Lord and His commandments but their works and their lives evidence minds that deny God. Because what they do is offensive, disobedient, and wicked.

Apparently they love and desire their sins more than the Lord's way because they display no passion, no delight, no enthusiasm and no desire for the Lord or the Lord's way: Note: "reprobate" means wicked and worthless

▶ 15. Unto the pure all things are pure: but unto them that are defiled and unbelieving is nothing pure; but even their mind and conscience is defiled.

16. They profess that they know God; but in works they deny him, being abominable, and disobedient, and unto every good work reprobate.

Titus 1: 15-16

You have one of two choices when the word of the Lord "Convicts" a person. Denying the Lord and choosing to continue in sin brings about reprobate (wicked/worthless).

After Apostle Stephen preached and they were "cut to the heart" they chose to reject the Lord and continue in their sin whereas when Peter preached after Pentecost about three thousand souls gladly received His word and were baptized.

So maybe you have some work to do here. You are not alone. This is the work for all of us Christians. We need to focus and hold in our hearts good things.

Again be encouraged because it is the power of the Lord the Higher Power the Creator God, the Good Heavenly Father, the Holy One, the Redeemer that overcomes on our behalf! As Apostle John writes in a letter:

Note: "he that is in you" is the Lord.
Note: "he that is in the world" is Satan.

▶ Ye are of God, little children, and have overcome them: because greater is he that is in you, than he that is in the world.

1 John 4:4

He overcomes on our behalf and provides for us. Great is our reward and blessings here on earth as well as our reward and blessings to come in heaven as it is the will of Lord, the Good Heavenly Father, the Creator God of the Universe, the Higher

CHAPTER 2
What you hold in your heart
that is what you attract.

Power, the Redeemer to give us such superior good things that are far better than what we could ever give one another, better than what we could ever obtain.

We need to conform our desires to acceptable desires of the Lord, the Higher Power the Creator God, the Good Heavenly Father, the Holy One, the Redeemer, so that He can release the blessings described above in Deuteronomy 28: 1-14.

Re-read Deuteronomy 28: 1-14, The Lord's Blessings. The Lord's promise is for those that follow the Lord's commandments that His blessings shall come on thee, and "overtake thee" Deuteronomy 28: 2.

The Lord's desire is to provide us good blessings that "overtake thee," the Deuteronomy 28: 2 blessings.
Be aware that we can limit, reduce or decrease our blessings!

A Giving Heart

Another example of the principles of what you hold in your heart is what you attract is in a "giving heart." The Lord provides you with the same measure of blessings that you mete out (measure out) in giving to others!

▶ Give, and it shall be given unto you; good measure, pressed down, and shaken together, and running over, shall men give into your bosom. For with the same measure that ye mete withal it shall be measured to you again.

Luke 6:38

The Lord gives you the same measure of blessings, which you mete out (measure out) in giving to others!
Note: Take caution. Being taken advantage of is not giving. It is being beguiled, swindled and cheated.

The Blessings are from the Lord not from man. Abraham trusted in the Lord and refused the king of Sodom's offer of the spoils of victory. Abraham relied on the promise and covenant of God.

Note: shoelatchet is an old word for shoelace.

▶ That I will not take from a thread even to a shoelatchet, and that I will not take any thing that is thine, lest thou shouldest say, I have made Abram rich:

Genesis 14:23

Had Abraham taken the King's gift then after that it would not have been clear whether the Lord caused Abraham to prosper or whether it was the gift from the king of Sodom.

Think through giving and taking gifts, as it is a lot more involved than mostly one is aware.

Holding in one's heart is what one attracts. When one seeks heavenly treasures one Tunes in Heaven and as a result attracts blessings and treasures:

▶ 19. Lay not up for yourselves treasures upon earth, where moth and rust doth corrupt, and where thieves break through and steal:

20. But lay up for yourselves treasures in heaven, where neither moth nor rust doth corrupt, and where thieves do not break through nor steal:

21. For where your treasure is, there will your heart be also. Matthew 6:19-21

Money:
WARNING: We should not just desire money in itself. But desire in our hearts the good things then the Lord provides a

CHAPTER 2
What you hold in your heart
that is what you attract.

way to get the good things to us and so money is just one of the many ways for the Lord to fulfill the desires of the good things held in our heart.

▶ For the love of money is the root of all evil: which while some coveted after, they have erred from the faith, and pierced themselves through with many sorrows.

1 Timothy: 6-10

King David's psalm, Psalm 37, praises these precepts to trust, delight and commit one's way to the way of the Lord and assures receiving the desires of one's heart:

▶ 3. Trust in the Lord, and do good; so shalt thou dwell in the land, and verily thou shalt be fed.

4. Delight thyself also in the Lord: and he shall give thee the desires of thine heart.

Psalm 37: 3-4

Blessings, Protection & Curses Extends to Those Nearby:

Blessings, Protections & Curses extends to those nearby. The Good Blessings that one attracts, flows and benefits those nearby. And, in addition there is protection: anyone cheating or offending the one whom the Lord is blessing experiences difficulty, stress and deficiency.

This was the case with Jacob. Those near to Jacob were benefited. And those cheating and offending Jacob were negatively affected, specifically Laban.

In Genesis, Laban was the father-in-law of Jacob, as he was the father of Rachel and Leah who were the wives of Jacob. Jacob is the one who was later re-named Israel.

When Laban's sons accused Jacob of taking away all that was their father, Laban's. Jacob explained that his portion was "Blessed" for that reason the increase.

Jacob called Rachel and Leah to the field where he kept his flock. Jacob clarified to them that Laban, their father had cheated him out of wages over and over again. That he, Jacob had a dream and in the dream Jacob asked Laban to clarify his wages by either choosing speckled animals or ringstraked (streaked) animals as his wages. Then clearly the Lord blessed Jacob's portion with increase.

The account in Genesis of Jacob explaining to Rachel and Leah:

▶ 6. And ye know that with all my power I have served your father.

7. And your father hath deceived me, and changed my wages ten times; but God suffered him not to hurt me.

8. If he said thus, The speckled shall be thy wages; then all the cattle bare speckled: and if he said thus, The ringstraked shall be thy hire; then bare all the cattle ringstraked.

9. Thus God hath taken away the cattle of your father, and given them to me.

Genesis 31: 6-9

The Will of the Lord to give Blessings to Jacob could not be thwarted! Jacob received his Blessings!

Apostle Paul warns us to separate away from those who are disorderly, not walking in the way of the Lord:

▶ Now we command you, brethren, in the name of our Lord Jesus Christ, that ye withdraw yourselves from every brother

CHAPTER 2
What you hold in your heart
that is what you attract.

who walketh disorderly and not according to the tradition
which he received from us.

2 Thessalonians 3:6

Continue to read Tune-In Heaven to find out how the Lord,
God Almighty, the Protector, the Creator God of the
Universe, the Good Heavenly Father, the Higher Power, the
Holy One, the Redeemer thwarts evil to give you the good
desires of your heart.

He gives you the power to choose beliefs regardless of
whether the beliefs are understood as fact, supernatural or
theory. Choose beliefs that are consistent with the Word of
the Lord. These beliefs then shape our decisions to choose
which desires to hold in our heart and then there are the
follow-on blessings or consequences.

CHAPTER 3

~

EVIL THWARTED
JUSTICE/GOOD ACHIEVED

When evil is intended against you, then the Higher Power, the God of the universe, the Creator God, the Holy One, the Good Heavenly Father, the Redeemer that loves you, He thwarts the evil and brings about justice and makes good be achieved. He is our Protector, the Mighty One.

When evil is intended against you He redirects it back to sender and utterly destroys the evil or the Lord means it for good and brings it to pass to save you and many more people. He is our Protector, the Mighty One, He lets you enter into His Joy and gives you the desires of your heart and is wholly worthy. Tune-In Heaven. The Lord answers prayer!

The Higher Power, God Almighty, the Creator God, the Holy One, the Good Heavenly Father, the Redeemer, the Lord has the power to effect that which He please and it shall prosper where it is sent. As in Isaiah: •

▶ 10. For as the rain cometh down, and the snow from heaven, and returneth not thither, but watereth the earth, and maketh it bring forth and bud, that it may give seed to the sower, and bread to the eater:

11. So shall my word be that goeth forth out of my mouth: it shall not return unto me void, but it shall accomplish that which I please, and it shall prosper in the thing whereto I sent it.

Isaiah 55:10-11

When evil is intended against you The Higher Power, The Protector, God Almighty, the Creator God, the Holy One, the Redeemer, thwarts the evil and brings about justice and makes good be achieved.

Haman:

In the Book of Esther the Lord redirects back to Haman the evil he intended against Mordecai. Haman hung on the very gallows he built to hang the good man, Mordecai and many lives were saved:

In ancient Persia, Haman one of the top officials calculated a plot to kill all of the Jews living in Persia and hang Mordecai a Jew on gallows. Mordecai was a good man. Haman built gallows fifty cubits high (about 85 feet high) to hang Mordecai. But the events turned against Haman.

Unbeknownst to Haman the King's wife, Queen Esther herself was a Jew and Haman's evil intentions were thwarted and redirected back to sender, and Haman was hanged from the very same gallows Haman built with the intentions to hang Mordecai. The Jews were saved. Then afterwards Haman's ten sons died in battle trying to kill the Jews. Their dead bodies were hanged on the very same gallows.

(Esther 7-Esther 9).

CHAPTER 3
EVIL THWARTED
JUSTICE/GOOD ACHIEVED

Joseph

When evil is intended against you The Higher Power, God Almighty, the Protector, the Creator God, the Holy One, the Good Heavenly Father, the Redeemer thwarts the evil and brings about justice and makes good be achieved.

In the Book of Genesis the Lord redirects the evil that was intended against Joseph by his brothers and all Israel was saved.

Jacob, who was renamed Israel, the founding father of ancient Israel, had twelve sons. Joseph was one of the sons. Ten of the other sons were very jealous of Joseph.

The father, Jacob loved Joseph more than his other sons. The father, Jacob gave Joseph a beautiful coat of many colors. Joseph had symbolic dreams that his brothers bowed to him. Even the Sun, Moon and stars bowed to Joseph in his dreams, which symbolically translates that his family was bowing to him. He told his brothers these dreams and it fueled the fire of jealousy!

Then one day Joseph met up with his brothers out in the fields tending the sheep. His brothers confronted him, pulled off of him his coat of many colors, cast him into a pit then sold him as a slave to merchants that were traveling by these ten sons of Israel.

The merchants sold Joseph as a slave in Egypt. He performed good work for his master, Potiphar. But Joseph was falsely accused of a crime and was put into a prison.

But events turn in Joseph's favor when he is brought up from the prison to be in front of Pharaoh to interpret a dream.

Joseph interpreted Pharaoh's dream: "there will be seven years of bounty followed by seven years of famine." Pharaoh was very impressed with Joseph's dream interpretation.

Pharaoh was so impressed that he appointed Joseph to a position in the government of Egypt putting him in charge of storing food for the upcoming hard times.

Then after the seven years of bounty passed the famine came about. The brothers of Joseph showed up in Egypt looking for food. Joseph recognized his brothers. His brothers did not recognize Joseph as their brother. They only saw Joseph as Pharaoh's powerful authority. This is very compelling and heartfelt: Joseph reveals himself to his brothers.

But as for you, ye thought evil against me; but God meant it unto good, to bring to pass, as it is this day, to save much people alive.

Joseph

Joseph 's brothers were in fear when they learned that they were in front of their brother Joseph the highest officer in Egypt, the one whom they sold into slavery.

Then they were afraid because of Joseph's powerful position in Egypt. They were afraid of vengeance on them for what they had done to Joseph: throwing Joseph into a pit then selling him as a slave. However, Joseph has forgiveness in his heart and causes the bounty of Egypt to be shared with his family and all Israel was saved. Joseph revealed to his brothers that what they "meant for evil that the Lord meant for good":

▶ But as for you, ye thought evil against me; but God meant it unto good, to bring to pass, as it is this day, to save much people alive.

Genesis 50:20

Conviction.

When evil was intended against Joseph and Mordecai the Lord thwarted the evil and brought about justice and good was achieved.

Joseph's brothers in Egypt expressed their remorse and repented over their previous evil intensions against their own brother Joseph. They were "convicted" in their hearts. They were very sorry for what they had done to Joseph, similarly as to those that were convicted when Apostle Peter preached. Then all of Joseph's brothers, their families and their father, Isaiah moved into Egypt and were treated special by the Pharaoh. All of Israel was saved from the famine and prospered!

Whereas, neither Haman nor any of his ten (10) sons are accounted for as repented. In The Book of Esther, in the Old Testament of the Bible it is abundantly clear that Haman was made fully aware of the good deeds of Mordecai, such as Mordecai uncovering a plot to assassinate the king, and the king was saved. At one point Haman led the king's own horse, with Mordecai sitting on the horse through the city square, shouting, "This is what the king does for someone he wishes to honor!"

But nowhere in The Book of Esther was Haman or any of his sons accounted for as remorseful. Just like when Apostle Stephen preached those that were "convicted" gnashed their teeth, and continued in their sin. Haman was hanged on the gallows he had built to hang Mordecai.

And, Haman's ten (10) sons after they were killed then their bodies were hanged on those same gallows.

The Lord is our Protector, the Higher Power, the Mighty One, the Good Heavenly Father, the Redeemer. He redirects evil back to sender then utterly destroys the evil or He means it for good and brings it to pass to save you and many more people. He is our Protector, the Mighty One, He lets you enter into His Joy and gives you the desires of your heart and is wholly worthy. The Lord answers prayer!

Be aware when choices are presented, process the information and make a decision to obey the Lord's Commandments and Tune-In Heaven. Develop a personal relationship with the Higher Power, the Protector, God Almighty, the Good Heavenly Father, the Holy One, the Creator God, the Redeemer and enter into His Joy!

God Almighty, the Higher Power the Creator God, the Holy One, the Redeemer, the Lord is this power to effect that which He pleases and it shall prosper where it is sent.

The Lord's promise of protection as found in Isaiah:

▶ No weapon that is formed against thee shall prosper; and every tongue that shall rise against thee in judgment thou shalt condemn. This is the heritage of the servants of the Lord, and their righteousness is of me, saith the Lord.

Isaiah 54:17

The Lord's promise of protection in a song of King David:

▶ 14. The wicked have drawn out the sword, and have bent their bow, to cast down the poor and needy, and to slay such as be of upright conversation.

15. Their sword shall enter into their own heart, and their bows shall be broken.

Psalm 37: 14-15

The Higher Power, God Almighty, the Protector, the Good Heavenly Father, the Holy One, the Redeemer has the power to thwart evil and achieve good. No where else is the evidence so clear of evil being thwarted and justice and good achieved than when Jesus Christ of Nazareth, the Higher Power, the Creator God, the Holy One, the God Almighty, the Redeemer - walked on this earth.

When Jesus Christ of Nazareth, the Higher Power, the Creator God, the Holy One, God Almighty, the Redeemer - walked on this earth.

Jesus taught that from good comes good and from evil comes evil.

▶ 33. Either make the tree good, and his fruit good; or else make the tree corrupt, and his fruit corrupt: for the tree is known by his fruit.

34. O generation of vipers, how can ye, being evil, speak good things? for out of the abundance of the heart the mouth speaketh.

35. A good man out of the good treasure of the heart bringeth forth good things: and an evil man out of the evil treasure bringeth forth evil things.

Matthew 12: 33-35

Multitudes recognized Jesus as the Higher Power, the God Almighty, the Protector, the Creator God, the Holy One, the Redeemer when he walked on this earth. But others missed it or purposefully denied Him:

The scribes and Pharisees challenged the authenticity of Jesus and asked Him for proof by asking Him to show them a sign.

Now picture this: right in front of the eyes of the scribes and Pharisees, they are seeing Jesus Christ, the Higher Power, the Creator God, the Holy One, God Almighty, the Redeemer standing in front of them in plain view. Could they really just have not recognized Him?

Meanwhile, also in front of the Pharisees were the multitudes that had absolutely recognized Him and would testify as such.

"Throng" of people

Everywhere Jesus went there was a "throng" of people pressing in on Him from every side. A throng of people means a huge multitude of people. And, everywhere Jesus went He performed miracles, healing the sick, casting out demons and performed wonders like feeding multitudes and walking on the water. They all had witnessed His miracles.

Jesus "healed them all." All as in all! The Healings were not sporadic. Everyone was healed! As recorded in the Gospel of Mathew:

▶ ... and great multitudes followed him, and he healed them all;

Matthew 12:15

How many Healings, Demon's Expelled and things of Wonder were done by Jesus? Apostle John explains:

▶ And there are also many other things which Jesus did, the which, if they should be written every one, I suppose that even the world itself could not contain the books that should be written. Amen.

John 21: 25

In this context the scribes and Pharisees ask Jesus for proof by showing a sign. How could anyone miss it! Apparently these scribes and Pharisees must have intentionally not recognized Jesus.

Jesus knows the hearts of man. So when they asked Him to show a sign He replies as detailed in the Gospel of Matthew: Note: the word generation also means other types of groupings of people as well, not just an age group.

▶ 38. Then certain of the scribes and of the Pharisees answered, saying, Master, we would see a sign from thee.

39. But he answered and said unto them, An evil and adulterous generation seeketh after a sign; and there shall no sign be given to it, but the sign of the prophet Jonas:

40. For as Jonas was three days and three nights in the whale's belly; so shall the Son of man be three days and three nights in the heart of the earth.

Matthew 12: 38-40

Comparing the Jonas experience to Jesus:

Jonas was swallowed by the whale. Then Jonas was spewed out after three (3) days. Jesus was crucified on the cross to death, buried in a tomb then Jesus rose on the third day. That was the promised sign. Wow!

How many Miracles and Wonders did Jesus perform?

The answer is the number of healings, casting out evil spirits and wonders were too many too document! The Apostle John reported about the multitude of the miracles and wonders that Jesus performed in the Gospel of John:

▶ And there are also many other things which Jesus did, the which, if they should be written every one, I suppose that even the world itself could not contain the books that should be written. Amen.

John 21:25

Jesus always had the Power to avoid the Cross:
He Laid down His Life!

Evidenced on the first day of His Ministry Jesus miraculously avoids the loss of His Life:

Jesus announced the beginning of His ministry on the Sabbath Day in the synagogue in Nazareth, the city where Jesus had grown-up. Jesus was rejected by those of the synagogue and they led him to the edge of a cliff to throw Him down. But Jesus miraculously just turns into the crowd, walks through the midst of the crowd and goes on His way!

▶ 28. And all they in the synagogue, when they heard these things, were filled with wrath,

29. And rose up, and thrust him out of the city, and led him unto the brow of the hill whereon their city was built, that they might cast him down headlong.

30. But he passing through the midst of them went his way,

Luke 4: 28-30

The first day of His Mission was clearly too soon to fulfill His scriptural sacrificial death. Jesus later on allowed Himself to be taken at the Garden of Gethsemane, then to the Cross.

At the Garden of Gethsemane, just prior to the Cross, the power of Jesus was evidenced when Jesus spoke "I am He" and Roman Soldiers were knocked down.

A number of Roman Soldiers were knocked down to the ground by the voice of Jesus in the Garden of Gethsemane out of a band of men and officers from the chief priests and Pharisees, also along, present was Judas, men who had came with lanterns and torches and weapons to take Jesus.

▶ As soon then as he had said unto them, I am he, they went backward, and fell to the ground.

John 18:6

He allowed Himself to be taken from the Garden of Gethsemane, be tried, sentenced and hung on the Cross.

On the cross Jesus laid down His life. He bowed His head and gave up the ghost as it is recorded in the Gospel of John:

▶ ... He said, It is finished: and he bowed his head, and gave up the ghost.

John 19:30

The Miracle of the Resurrection of Jesus from the Dead.

Jesus has Risen:

Witnesses of the Resurrection

The empty tomb was discovered. Mary Magdalene and the Disciples discovered the empty tomb. Two angels where in the tomb. Jesus in His resurrected body speaks with Mary Magdalene to not touch Him "as for I am not yet ascended to my Father." The full account is in John 20:1-18

In the Gospel of Mark, on the third day, three women see the stone had been rolled away and enter the sepulcher (tomb):

▶ 5. And entering into the sepulcher, they saw a young man sitting on the right side, clothed in a long white garment; and they were affrighted.

6. And he saith unto them, Be not affrighted: Ye seek Jesus of Nazareth, which was crucified: he is risen; he is not here: behold the place where they laid him.

Mark 16:5-6

As recorded in the Gospel of Matthew, Resurrection morning:

▶ 5. And the angel answered and said unto the women, Fear not ye: for I know that ye seek Jesus, which was crucified.

6. He is not here: for he is risen, as he said. Come, see the place where the Lord lay.

7. And go quickly, and tell his disciples that he is risen from the dead; and, behold, he goeth before you into Galilee; there shall ye see him: lo, I have told you.

Matthew 28:5-7

Resurrection morning as recorded in Luke:

▶ 1. Now upon the first day of the week, very early in the morning, they came unto the sepulchre, bringing the spices which they had prepared, and certain others with them.

2. And they found the stone rolled away from the sepulchre.

3. And they entered in, and found not the body of the Lord Jesus.

4. And it came to pass, as they were much perplexed thereabout, behold, two men stood by them in shining garments:

5. And as they were afraid, and bowed down their faces to the earth, they said unto them, Why seek ye the living among the dead?

6. He is not here, but is risen: remember how he spake unto you when he was yet in Galilee,

7. Saying, The Son of man must be delivered into the hands of sinful men, and be crucified, and the third day rise again.

8. And they remembered his words,

9. And returned from the sepulchre, and told all these things unto the eleven, and to all the rest.

Luke 24:1-9

Appearances of the Resurrected Jesus.

The Disciples meet Jesus on a Mountain after He resurrects from the dead:

▶ 16. Then the eleven disciples went away into Galilee, into a mountain where Jesus had appointed them.

17. And when they saw him, they worshipped him: but some doubted.

18. And Jesus came and spake unto them, saying, All power is given unto me in heaven and in earth.

Matthew 28:16-18

The Apostle John records in the Gospel of John the resurrected Jesus appearing in their midst:

▶ 19. Then the same day at evening, being the first day of the week, when the doors were shut where the disciples were assembled for fear of the Jews, came Jesus and stood in the midst, and saith unto them, Peace be unto you.

20. And when he had so said, he shewed unto them his hands and his side. Then were the disciples glad, when they saw the Lord.

21. Then said Jesus to them again, Peace be unto you: as my Father hath sent me, even so send I you.

22. And when he had said this, he breathed on them, and saith unto them, Receive ye the Holy Ghost:

23. Whose soever sins ye remit, they are remitted unto them; and whose soever sins ye retain, they are retained.

24. But Thomas, one of the twelve, called Didymus, was not with them when Jesus came.

John 20:19-24

Then about eight (8) days later the Resurrected Jesus appears again in their midst and this time Thomas was with them. This is the account of the "Doubting Thomas."

The Disciple Thomas earlier had told the others that the only way Thomas would believe such a thing like that Jesus resurrected from the dead was that he, Thomas would have to personally thrust his fingers through the holes in the hands and side of Jesus.

Well that is actually, exactly then what happened. The Resurrected Jesus appeared in their midst and instructed Thomas to thrust his fingers into the holes of His hands and His side so that Thomas would believe:

▶ 26. And after eight days again his disciples were within, and Thomas with them: then came Jesus, the doors being shut, and stood in the midst, and said, Peace be unto you.

27. Then saith he to Thomas, Reach hither thy finger, and behold my hands; and reach hither thy hand, and thrust it into my side: and be not faithless, but believing.

28. And Thomas answered and said unto him, My Lord and my God.

29. Jesus saith unto him, Thomas, because thou hast seen me, thou hast believed: blessed are they that have not seen, and yet have believed.

John 20: 26-29

Apostle Paul testifies of 500 witnesses to the Resurrected Jesus:

The Apostle Paul was testifying to the Corinthians how that Jesus died for our sins according to the scriptures in a letter to the Corinthians that includes a list of witnesses to the Resurrected Jesus.

The list cites five hundred (500) at one time having witnessed the Resurrect Jesus:

Note: Cephas is another name for Apostle Peter.
Note: Fallen asleep of course means here that they died.

▶ 4. And that he was buried, and that he rose again the third day according to the scriptures:

5. And that he was seen of Cephas, then of the twelve:

6. After that, he was seen of above five hundred brethren at once; of whom the greater part remain unto this present, but some are fallen asleep.

7. After that, he was seen of James; then of all the apostles.

8. And last of all he was seen of me also, as of one born out of due time.

1 Corinthians 15: 4 -8

The Bible records other eyewitness accounts of Jesus after the resurrection. For example two (2) traveling men:

Two men were on the way to a village named Emmaus. One of the men was Cleopas. They were joined along the way with the Resurrected Jesus. But they did not recognize Jesus. They received a Bible lesson from Jesus, Himself explaining that the suffering, death, and Resurrection fulfilled the Old Testament Scriptures.

As they neared their destination they stopped and broke bread with Jesus, then His identity was revealed to them and He vanished. Wow!

What an encounter to be personally taught scripture by Jesus Christ of Nazareth, the Higher Power, the Creator God, the Holy One, God Almighty, the Redeemer.

This encounter of the Resurrected Jesus with two (2) travelers on their way to the village of Emmaus is recorded in the Gospel of Luke:

▶ 13. And, behold, two of them went that same day to a village called Emmaus, which was from Jerusalem about threescore furlongs.

14. And they talked together of all these things which had happened.

15. And it came to pass, that, while they communed together and reasoned, Jesus himself drew near, and went with them.

16. But their eyes were holden that they should not know him.

17. And he said unto them, What manner of communications are these that ye have one to another, as ye walk, and are sad?

18. And the one of them, whose name was Cleopas, answering said unto him, Art thou only a stranger in Jerusalem, and hast not known the things which are come to pass there in these days?

19. And he said unto them, What things? And they said unto him, Concerning Jesus of Nazareth, which was a prophet mighty in deed and word before God and all the people:

20. And how the chief priests and our rulers delivered him to be condemned to death, and have crucified him.

21. But we trusted that it had been he which should have redeemed Israel: and beside all this, to day is the third day since these things were done.

22. Yea, and certain women also of our company made us astonished, which were early at the sepulchre;

23. And when they found not his body, they came, saying, that they had also seen a vision of angels, which said that he was alive.

24. And certain of them which were with us went to the sepulchre, and found it even so as the women had said: but him they saw not.

25. Then he said unto them, O fools, and slow of heart to believe all that the prophets have spoken:

26. Ought not Christ to have suffered these things, and to enter into his glory?

27. And beginning at Moses and all the prophets, he expounded unto them in all the scriptures the things concerning himself.

28. And they drew nigh unto the village, whither they went: and he made as though he would have gone further.

29. But they constrained him, saying, Abide with us: for it is toward evening, and the day is far spent. And he went in to tarry with them.

30. And it came to pass, as he sat at meat with them, he took bread, and blessed it, and brake, and gave to them.

31. And their eyes were opened, and they knew him; and he vanished out of their sight.

32. And they said one to another, Did not our heart burn within us, while he talked with us by the way, and while he opened to us the scriptures?

Luke 24: 13-32

Luke is the author of the Gospel of Luke who is also the author of the Acts of the Apostles, known as "Acts," In Acts is attested to infallible proofs, being seen of them for forty (40) days of the Resurrected Jesus. The Resurrected Jesus appeared for forty (40) days and was witnessed by many performing infallible proofs as recorded in Acts:

▶ 2. Until the day in which he was taken up, after that he through the Holy Ghost had given commandments unto the apostles whom he had chosen:

3. To whom also he shewed himself alive after his passion by many infallible proofs, being seen of them forty days, and speaking of the things pertaining to the kingdom of God:

Acts 1: 2-3

Ascension of Jesus to Heaven.

Jesus spoke to the Disciples in His Resurrected Body then Ascended:

▶ 9. And when he had spoken these things, while they beheld, he was taken up; and a cloud received him out of their sight.

10. And while they looked stedfastly toward heaven as he went up, behold, two men stood by them in white apparel;

11. Which also said, Ye men of Galilee, why stand ye gazing up into heaven? this same Jesus, which is taken up from you into heaven, shall so come in like manner as ye have seen him go into heaven.

Acts 1: 9-11

Jesus Miracles Performed, The Raising of the Dead, Healing Miracles and Casting out Evil Spirits and Signs and Wonders

List of the Miracles and Wonders of Jesus Found in the New Testament:

The Ultimate Miracle - Raising the Dead!

Jesus Christ raised three (3) different individuals from the dead:

Jesus Raised from the Dead a Daughter of a Ruler

(Matthew 9:18-19, 23-26)

Jesus Raised from the Dead a Widow's Son

(Luke 7:11-17)

Jesus Raised Lazarus from the Dead, the brother of Mary, she was the one whom had anointed the Lord with ointment and wiped the feet of the Lord with her hair.
(John 11:1-44)

Healing Miracles and Casting out Evil Spirits

Jesus healed a leper.
(Matthew 8:1-4)

Jesus healed two (2) blind men
(Matthew 9:27-31)

Jesus cast out a devil, and then a mute man could speak.
(Matthew 9:32-33)

Jesus healed the daughter of a Canaanite woman after she responded "dogs eat of the crumbs which fall from their masters' table after Jesus told her He came for the sheep of Israel.

(Matthew 15:21-28)

Jesus casts out an unclean spirit from of a man in the synagogue.

(Mark 1:23-28)

Jesus healed a deaf boy and his speech.

(Mark 7:31-37)

Jesus heals a blind man.

(Mark 8:22-26)

Jesus healed the mother of Peter's wife of a great fever.

(Luke 4:38-39)

Jesus healed a man of palsy

(Luke 5:17-26)

Jesus healed a man with a withered hand on the Sabbath.

(Luke 6:6-10)

Jesus healed the Roman centurion's servant at a distance.

(Luke 7:1-10)

CHAPTER 3
EVIL THWARTED
JUSTICE/GOOD ACHIEVED

Jesus cast out devils from a man, the devils entered into a herd of swine, and then the herd of swine violently ran into the lake where they drown. The devils name were Legion because there were many devils.

(Luke 8:26-39)

Jesus healed a Woman having an issue of blood twelve years.

(Luke 8:43-48)

Jesus restored a boy by casting out an unclean spirit.

(Luke 9:37-43)

Jesus cast out a devil, and then a mute man could speak.

(Luke 11:14)

Jesus was teaching on the Sabbath in the synagogue and healed a woman who stood straight after she was "bowed together for eighteen (18) years.

(Luke 13:10-13)

Jesus on the Sabbath healed a man with dropsy.

(Luke 14:1-4)

Jesus healed ten (10) lepers, one (1) came back and gave thanks.

(Luke 17:11-19)

Jesus cured a blind beggar.

(Luke 18:35-43)

Jesus restored the ear of a Roman soldier. When the Roman soldiers came to get Jesus one of the Disciples whacked off an ear of a soldier. Jesus restored the soldier's ear.

(Luke 22:50-51)

Jesus spoke the son's healing to the father then at that very hour the boy was healed from a distance.

(John 4:43-54)

Jesus told the man to pick-up his bed and walk at a pool at Bethesda and the man was healed of an infirmity suffered for thirty-eight (38) years.

(John 5:1-15)

Jesus healed a blind beggar, who had been blind since birth.

(John 9:1-12)

Signs and Wonders

Jesus commanded Peter to catch a fish, open its mouth then take out the coin and pay the tax.

(Matthew 17:24-27)

Jesus rebuked the wind and the raging water then the sea calmed down while the Disciples and Jesus were onboard a boat.

(Mark 4:35-41)

Jesus fed 5,000 men and their families with five (5) loafs of bread and two (2) fish.

(Mark 6:30-44)

The disciples from with inside a boat witnessed Jesus walking on the Sea.

(Mark 6:45-52)

Jesus fed 4,000 men and families with seven (7) loafs of bread.

(Mark 8:1-10)

Jesus cursed a fig tree that had no figs then the next day it had withered.

(Mark 11:11-14, 20-26)

Jesus commanded Peter to cast the net and Peter obeyed and enclosed a large multitude of fish. Peter and Andrew his brother and the other fishermen James, and John forsook all and became disciples of Jesus.

(Luke 5:1-11)

Jesus turned the water into wine at the marriage in Cana. (John 2:1-11)

A number of Roman Soldiers were knocked down to the ground by the voice of Jesus in the Garden of Gethsemane out of a band of men and officers from the chief priests and Pharisees, also along was Judas who had came with lanterns and torches and weapons to take Jesus.

▶ As soon then as he had said unto them, I am he, they went backward, and fell to the ground.

John 18:6

The third time that Jesus showed himself to His Disciples after He had risen from the dead the Disciples were fishing and caught a great multitude of fish.

(John 21:1-14)

Earthquake:

Moments after Jesus Died on the Cross there was an earthquake, the veil (curtain) of the temple was torn from the top to the bottom (rent means torn, twain means two), the graves opened and the dead (those who slept) arose and appeared to many in Jerusalem!

▶ 50. Jesus, when he had cried again with a loud voice, yielded up the ghost.

51. And, behold, the veil of the temple was rent in twain from the top to the bottom; and the earth did quake, and the rocks rent;

52. And the graves were opened; and many bodies of the saints which slept arose,

53. And came out of the graves after his resurrection, and went into the holy city, and appeared unto many.

Matthew 27:50-53

John concludes the Gospel of John with the following:

▶ 30. And many other signs truly did Jesus in the presence of his disciples, which are not written in this book:

31. But these are written, that ye might believe that Jesus is the Christ, the Son of God; and that believing ye might have life through his name.

John 20: 30-31

.

CHAPTER 4

~

Come Into a
Personal Relationship
With the Higher Power
The Holy One, the Redeemer

You can have a personal relationship with the Higher Power, the God of the Universe, the Creator God, the Holy One, the Redeemer. He is now reaching out to you as the prophet Isaiah declares: "God's arms are stretched out still." The stretched out arms of Jesus are now reaching out to you to enter into His Joy and receive His Blessings, Prosperity and Protection.

You can develop a personal relationship with God Almighty, the Higher Power, the Holy One, the Creator God, the Redeemer. Commit your way to the Lord and Obey the Lord's Commandments and Tune-In Heaven.

▶ And thou shalt love the Lord thy God with all thy heart, and with all thy soul, and with all thy mind, and with all thy strength: this is the first commandment.
Mark 12:30

Remember to love the Lord is to keep his commandments:

▶ If ye love me, keep my commandments.
John 14:15

▶ And we know that all things work together for good to them that love God, to them who are the called according to his purpose.

Romans 8:28

In the Bible we can find instructions from those who trusted in the Lord, committed their way to the Lord and developed a personal relationship with the Higher Power, the Creator God, the Redeemer and they received His Joy, Blessings, Prosperity and Protection. Here are examples for us to follow:

King David's praises these precepts to trust, delight (no complaining) and commit one's way to the ways of the Lord, which assures receiving the desires of one's heart. The Lord will bring upon righteousness. Evildoers will be cut off. Those that wait upon the Lord shall inherit the earth:

▶3. Trust in the Lord, and do good; so shalt thou dwell in the land, and verily thou shalt be fed.

4. Delight thyself also in the Lord: and he shall give thee the desires of thine heart.

5. Commit thy way unto the Lord; trust also in him; and he shall bring it to pass.

6. And he shall bring forth thy righteousness as the light, and thy judgment as the noonday.

7. Rest in the Lord, and wait patiently for him: fret not thyself because of him who prospereth in his way, because of the man who bringeth wicked devices to pass.

8. Cease from anger, and forsake wrath: fret not thyself in any wise to do evil.

9. For evildoers shall be cut off: but those that wait upon the Lord, they shall inherit the earth.

Psalm 37:3-9

To have a personal relationship with the Lord, to know the Lord, the Apostle Paul provides insight into the mind of the Lord. Paul asks: Who could provide the Lord with advice or provide credit so that God would have to repay?

Paul's letter to the Romans illustrates the Lord's knowledge wisdom, judgments and mind are beyond our understanding.

▶ 33. O the depth of the riches both of the wisdom and knowledge of God! How unsearchable are his judgments, and his ways past finding out!

34. For who hath known the mind of the Lord? or who hath been his counsellor?

35. Or who hath first given to him, and it shall be recompensed unto him again?

36. For of him, and through him, and to him, are all things: to whom be glory for ever. Amen.

Romans 11:33-36

Also, No Complaining: Apostle Paul warns against complaining as he compares people as pots and the Lord as the potter who makes different pots on the potter's wheel:

▶ 20. ... Shall the thing formed say to him that formed it, Why hast thou made me thus?

21.Hath not the potter power over the clay, of the same lump to make one vessel unto honour, and another unto dishonour?

22. What if God, willing to shew his wrath, and to make his power known, endured with much longsuffering the vessels of wrath fitted to destruction:

23. And that he might make known the riches of his glory on the vessels of mercy, which he had afore prepared unto glory

Romans 9: 20-23

Also the Prophet Isaiah warns not to complain to the Lord about our purpose for which we were made in comparing people as pots and Lord as the pot maker:

▶9. Woe unto him that striveth with his Maker! Let the potsherd strive with the potsherds of the earth. Shall the clay say to him that fashioneth it, What makest thou? or thy work, He hath no hands?
Isaiah 45:9

To have a personal relationship with the Lord we desire to know the ways of the Lord. In the book of Daniel we learn of the great extent that the Lord and His Heavenly Host of Angels underwent to answer the prayer of Daniel.
Praise God! Thank you Jesus!

In answer to Daniel's prayer the Lord sent to Daniel an angel. The "prince of the kingdom of Persia" (a demon or Satan) restrained the Lord's angel. Then Michael a prince of the Lord, possible an angel, or maybe as many believe is that Michael is Jesus in the Old Testament, came and detained the "prince of Persia" so that the Lord's first angel could go to Daniel to: "make thee understand what shall befall thy people in the latter days." Wow!

▶10. And, behold, an hand touched me, which set me upon my knees and upon the palms of my hands.

11. And he said unto me, O Daniel, a man greatly beloved, understand the words that I speak unto thee, and stand upright: for unto thee am I now sent. And when he had spoken this word unto me, I stood trembling.

12. Then said he unto me, Fear not, Daniel: for from the first day that thou didst set thine heart to understand, and to chasten thyself before thy God, thy words were heard, and I am come for thy words.

13. But the prince of the kingdom of Persia withstood me one and twenty days: but, lo, Michael, one of the chief princes, came to help me; and I remained there with the kings of Persia.

14. Now I am come to make thee understand what shall befall thy people in the latter days: for yet the vision is for many days.
Daniel 10: 10-14

Sin.
So then We have this Problem called Sin.

▶ As it is written, There is none righteous, no, not one:

Romans 3:10

Good thoughts attract that which is good: Blessings, the Joy of the Lord, and plays the mainstream share in the development of a personal relationship with the Higher Power, the Creator God, the Redeemer and receiving His Joy, Blessings, Prosperity and Protection.

To have a personal relationship with the Lord is to know these precepts to trust, delight (no complaining) and commit one's way to the ways of the Lord (following His Commandments) or, otherwise, disobeying the Lord is sin. Sin hinders us from knowing the Lord.

Jesus Fulfills the Law. Jesus is not a Free Pass to Sin!
When Jesus came He Fulfilled the law. Jesus made it known that the law would be here until the last days. Many say in error that the law was nailed to the cross with Christ. This is a lie from Satan. Do not believe such a lie. It is not Biblical.

Jesus clearly explains that the law is going to be with us and we are required to obey the law, even required to obey the least of the Commandments. The Gospel of Matthew:

▶ 17. Think not that I am come to destroy the law, or the prophets: I am not come to destroy, but to fulfil.

18. For verily I say unto you, Till heaven and earth pass, one jot or one tittle shall in no wise pass from the law, till all be fulfilled.

19. Whosoever therefore shall break one of these least commandments, and shall teach men so, he shall be called the least in the kingdom of heaven: but whosoever shall do and teach them, the same shall be called great in the kingdom of heaven.

Matthew 5: 17-19

Jesus explained the connection between anger and murder and the connection between lust and adultery.

Anger

Note: Raca means empty-headed, stupid – like an "air-head."

▶ 21. Ye have heard that it was said by them of old time, Thou shalt not kill; and whosoever shall kill shall be in danger of the judgment:

22. But I say unto you, That whosoever is angry with his brother without a cause shall be in danger of the judgment: and whosoever shall say to his brother, Raca, shall be in danger of the council: but whosoever shall say, Thou fool, shall be in danger of hell fire.

Matthew 5: 21-22

CHAPTER 4
Personal Relationship
With the Higher Power

Lust

▶ 27. Ye have heard that it was said by them of old time, Thou shalt not commit adultery:

28. But I say unto you, That whosoever looketh on a woman to lust after her hath committed adultery with her already in his heart.

Matthew 5:27-28

It starts in your mind. You feel convicted. You make a choice. It travels to your heart. What you hold in your heart is what you attract. If you choose evil - you attract evil.

If you get angry most likely you will not commit murder. But anger attracts evil generally. Anger does not attract blessings it repels blessings. Similarly, lusting with one's eyes does not necessarily mean that adultery will follow. But blessings are repelled. Evil attracts evil generally. You get more evil.

Anger and lust are sins. Complaining is a sin as well. When one complains one is finding faults with one's own gifts. When one is not satisfied with one's gifts the next step is to look at the gifts of others. Complaining may not necessarily lead to jealously or coveting the gifts of others. But blessings are repelled. Jesus taught that evil begets evil. Evil attracts more evil and blessings are repelled.

Good thoughts are first in the process to attract His Joy, Blessings, Prosperity and Protection. And, plays the mainstream share in the development of a personal relationship with the Higher Power, the Creator God, the Redeemer.

Trust in the Lord and commit your ways to the Lord and follow His law. Otherwise, disobeying the Lord is sin. Sin hinders us from knowing the Lord and attracts evil.

The Lord Does Not Give Up On Us.

The Lord has given us the ability to make decisions. He has given us free choice. We choose to never give up on ourselves and commit our ways to the Lord, and then re-commit our ways to the Lord.

We sin and are remorseful, repentant and ashamed to the Lord. We are contrite and come to the Lord and He forgives our sin, as He knows our heart. We repeat, we repeat until we get it right. Eventually we overcome! Praise the Lord!

Find delight in following the Lord's commandments and love and thank the Lord for dying on the cross for our sins.

Control sin in your mind, before it reaches the heart, and before acting out sin. The Lord gave us the ability to choose. Choose what is right. And always do the right thing.
Find delight in the ways of the Lord.

The Lord explains to Cane to control his sin in Genesis.

The Lord accepted Abel's offering. But the Lord did not accept Cane's offering. The Lord instructed Cane that Cane knew what to do, and that he needed to do what is well. Then the Lord warns Cane that sin is at the door. That Cane needed to master the sin or the sin would rule over him. Also take note that Cain is complaining:
Note: countenance means face, or facial expression.

▶ 5. But unto Cain and to his offering he had not respect. And Cain was very wroth, and his countenance fell.

6. And the LORD said unto Cain, Why art thou wroth? and why is thy countenance fallen?

7. If thou doest well, shalt thou not be accepted? and if thou doest not well, sin lieth at the door. And unto thee shall be his desire, and thou shalt rule over him.

Genesis 4: 5-7

So then if the sin rules over one then that person becomes a servant of sin.

▶ Jesus answered them, Verily, verily, I say unto you, Whosoever committeth sin is the servant of sin.

John 8:34

Jesus Came to "Preach Deliverance to the Captives:"

The Gospel of Luke reports that Jesus was anointed concerning a variety of matters including to "Preach Deliverance to the Captives:

▶ The Spirit of the Lord is upon me, because he hath anointed me to preach the gospel to the poor; he hath sent me to heal the brokenhearted, to preach deliverance to the captives, and recovering of sight to the blind, to set at liberty them that are bruised.

Luke 4:18

Who are the "captives" that Jesus talks about?

Answer: Sinners. Sinners are captive to sin, servants of sin, ruled over by the evil one. Jesus came to set the sinner free.

The Struggle of Apostle Paul with Sin:

Apostle Paul writes of his own personal struggle with sin and his answer to call upon the name of the Lord to be saved in his letter the Romans.

By the way, it is encouraging for many Christians that even the Apostle Paul, the relentless advocate of Jesus Christ, struggled with sin just like the rest of us.

His struggle is truly heart-felt, as he sincerely desired to do what was right but apparently fell short.

Apostle Paul gave the answer, which in our hearts we all know: "to call upon the name of the Lord."

Apostle Paul's description of his own personal struggle with sin in his letter the Romans.

▶ 19. For the good that I would I do not: but the evil which I would not, that I do.

20. Now if I do that I would not, it is no more I that do it, but sin that dwelleth in me.

21. I find then a law, that, when I would do good, evil is present with me.

22. For I delight in the law of God after the inward man:

23. But I see another law in my members, warring against the law of my mind, and bringing me into captivity to the law of sin, which is in my members.

24. O wretched man that I am! Who shall deliver me from the body of this death?

Romans 7:19-24

▶ For whosoever shall call upon the name of the Lord shall be saved.
Romans 10:13

Apostle Paul warns to stay free of sin:

▶ Stand fast therefore in the liberty wherewith Christ hath made us free, and be not entangled again with the yoke of bondage.

Galatians 5:1

Be encouraged:

Be encouraged. For folks who are experiencing this for the first time, realizing that the Lord is truly powerful, able and is God Almighty. This is not a hard thing. The same Lord loves us. He is also the Good Heavenly Father desiring for us to enter into His Joy and receive His Blessings. He is a Personal God who is always here for us. Also He is the Redeemer.

He personally paid for our sins with His life. Along with His knowledge and the Lord promises, He encourages:

▶ And he said, The things which are impossible with men are possible with God.

Luke 18:27

▶ For my yoke is easy, and my burden is light.

Matthew 11:30

▶ The fear of the Lord is the beginning of knowledge: but fools despise wisdom and instruction.

Proverbs 1:7

▶ And Jesus looking upon them saith, with men it is impossible, but not with God: for with God all things are possible.

Mark 10:27

Prelude\Forward to The Sinner's Prayer.

The guidance is to call upon the name of the Lord and to repent. There is no named "Sinner's Prayer" in the Bible. Though, the Sinner's Prayer is real. It includes the Biblical guidance to call upon the name of the Lord and repent. There are many variations of the Sinner's Prayer. The fundaments: You need to call upon the name of the Lord and to repent.

Are you committed to making positive changes in your life that impact and connect you to receiving the Blessings of the Good Heavenly Father, the Protection of God Almighty, and entering into the Joy of the Lord, the Higher Power, the Creator God, the Holy One, the Redeemer?

Following the Lord is not a burden but a joy! We delight in the Lord's precepts. We find joy in following His commandments. The Lord instructs: "if you love me follow my commandments." John 14:15

Control the sin in your heart before it takes control and becomes your master.

You have choice all the time: The God given ability to make decisions. Always choose what is right and do the right thing. You do the right thing no matter what everyone else is doing around you. You are always required to do the right thing.

One suffers the consequences of sinful actions. You desired it. You acted the evil out. You get the evil consequences: The curses, frustration, confusion, loss, sorrow, heartaches even death are the consequences of sin/evil actions. These consequences are real. Also the patterns and cycles repeat. You get stuck.

How does it stop?
Answer: Call upon the name of the Lord and repent!

We serve a just God. So we need to be redeemed by a Savior.
The Lord suffered unto his death to redeem us. He took the
punishment we deserve to make us acceptable to a just God.

Some say, "Shout it out!" You do not need to "Shout it out."
That depends on you and your surroundings.
But of course it is ok to shout it out. It is up to you.

WARNING: This is private. You do not share what you hold
in your heart with others. As Jesus has warned us in the
Gospel of Matthew:
Note: Rend means to separate or tear into parts.

► Give not that which is holy unto the dogs, neither cast ye
your pearls before swine, lest they trample them under their
feet, and turn again and rend you.
Matthew 7:6

Not everyone will have encouraging words for the new
believer. There are ones who will "rend" the new believer.

The Lord's jurisdiction is the heart. It is always between you
and the Lord. First read through the Sinner's Prayer on the
next page, which is the Sinner's Prayer that I recommend.
Which I think is perfect. You decide. Make changes if you
like.

You certainly can personalize the Sinner's Prayer as it is
between you and the Lord. You just need the two
fundaments: Calling upon the name of the Lord and
repenting. Praise you Father, Son and Holy Spirit!

CHAPTER 4
Personal Relationship
With the Higher Power

If you are ready: call upon the name of the Lord and repent.

The Sinner's Prayer

Dear Jesus, I call upon Your name Jesus, God Almighty, the Good Heavenly Father, the Higher Power the Creator God, the God of the Universe, the Holy One, the Holy Spirit, the Redeemer, the God of Abraham, Isaac and Jacob.

Thank you for convicting me of sin, in my mind, in my heart and in my actions. You loved me while I was still in sin. I want to turn away from sin and commit my way to Your way, Lord and to trust in You, Lord. Please forgive me, I am genuinely sorry, I desire to do what is right from now on, help me avoid sinning again.

Good Heavenly Father, I need your help. Please save me from the bondage of sin, save me from the curses, frustration, confusion, loss, sorrow, heartaches, further consequences of sin/evil actions and end the repeating patterns and cycles.

I desire positive changes in my life, to receive the Blessings, and the Prosperity of the Good Heavenly Father, and the Protection of God Almighty, and the Joy of the Lord.

I believe that your son, Jesus Christ died for my sins, was resurrected from the dead, is alive, and hears my prayer. Please Jesus become the Lord of my life. Rule and reign in my heart from this day forward. Let Your Will be done through me. Holy Spirit come dwell in me to empower me to obey God's commandments.

In Jesus name I pray. Praise you Father, Son and Holy Spirit. Thank you Jesus!
Amen.

CHAPTER 5

~

Truth

At a minimum one cannot benefit from false doctrine. False doctrine is useless and it makes life appear fortuitous. As discussed earlier if one is using a phony bus schedule maybe one will catch a bus or maybe one will not catch a bus. We need to start with the Truth since the truth attracts the Blessings and the Joy of the Lord. Jesus is the Truth:

▶ Jesus saith unto him, I am the way, the truth, and the life: no man cometh unto the Father, but by me.

John 14:6

Jesus answered Pilate:

▶ To this end was I born, and for this cause came I into the world, that I should bear witness unto the truth. Every one that is of the truth heareth my voice."

John 18:37

When we hold the truth in our hearts then we are holding Jesus in our hearts. Satan is the author of lies. When we hold lies in our hearts we attract curses. Nothing good comes from evil. As we go through life false doctrines are being presented to us. This chapter is presented to put forward principal truths to serve as guidance to expose modern false doctrines.

When Jesus who is the "Truth" was tempted by Satan in the desert after forty (40) days of fasting, Jesus quoted scripture. Satan tempted Jesus "to turn the stones into bread."
Jesus answered as follows:

▶ But he answered and said, It is written, Man shall not live by bread alone, but by every word that proceedeth out of the mouth of God.

Matthew 4:4

Jesus testified, "It is written." Precisely "It is written" is written in Deuteronomy in the Bible. After Moses led the Hebrews out of Egypt, Moses recorded that man shall live by "every word that proceedeth out of the mouth of the LORD" in Deuteronomy:

▶ And he humbled thee, and suffered thee to hunger, and fed thee with manna, which thou knewest not, neither did thy fathers know; that he might make thee know that man doth not live by bread only, but by every word that proceedeth out of the mouth of the LORD doth man live.

Deuteronomy 8:3

How should we evaluate modern "scientific" doctrines that influence and shape our beliefs, which, shape our desires and shape our decisions to make choices?

Answer: Any doctrine that contradicts the Lord's Word, which is the Bible then that doctrine, is not truthful. You cannot benefit from false doctrine. As stated in Isaiah:

▶ To the law and to the testimony: if they speak not according to this word, it is because there is no light in them.

Isaiah 8:20

In other words if any doctrine, scientific or otherwise that is not according to "this word" the Bible, then it is evil "no light in them."

Realize that doctrines that contradict the Word of the Lord are false doctrines "no light in them," - not truth. It is a lie!

Apostle Paul explains there is value (profit) in analyzing all doctrine according to the Bible (the inspired word of God).

► All scripture is given by inspiration of God, and is profitable for doctrine, for reproof, for correction, for instruction in righteousness:

2 Timothy 3:16

If the doctrine is not according to the Bible it is not truthful! The value is in the determination regarding the righteousness, honesty and truthfulness of the doctrine.

Keep in mind the principles discussed in chapter 2, that what you desire in your heart is what the creator God of the universe, the Higher Power, the Holy One will give you or allow you to choose.

You will receive the consequences of what you hold in your heart. The consequences of your actions purely are the results of your choices, therefore Truth matters regarding outside influences since they shapes our beliefs. Our beliefs shape our desires and our decisions to make specific choices.

Cast out false teachings and capture the inspirations of the Lord, the Creator of the Universe, the Higher Spirit, the Holy One and hold them in your heart.

Truth Matters in the "Talents Parable" Taught by Jesus:

For an example where truth matters is in the parable of the "Talents" taught by Jesus. Two servants receive blessings and one servant receives a curse, from Matthew 25:14-30:

The Parable of the Talents:

<The Lord's Gifts:>

▶ 14. For the kingdom of heaven is as a man travelling into a far country, who called his own servants, and delivered unto them his goods.

15. And unto one he gave five talents, to another two, and to another one; to every man according to his several ability; and straightway took his journey.

16. Then he that had received the five talents went and traded with the same, and made them other five talents.

17. And likewise he that had received two, he also gained other two,

18. But he that had received one went and digged in the earth, and hid his lord's money.

<The Return of the Lord, response to the first and second servants:>

▶ 19. After a long time the lord of those servants cometh, and reckoneth with them.

20. And so he that had received five talents came and brought other five talents, saying, Lord, thou deliveredst unto me five talents: behold, I have gained beside them five talents more.

21. His lord said unto him, Well done, thou good and faithful servant: thou hast been faithful over a few things, I will make thee ruler over many things: enter thou into the joy of thy lord.

22. He also that had received two talents came and said, Lord, thou deliveredst unto me two talents: behold, I have gained two other talents beside them.

23. His lord said unto him, Well done, good and faithful servant; thou hast been faithful over a few things, I will make thee ruler over many things: enter thou into the joy of thy lord.

<The Return of the Lord, response to the third servants:>

▶ 24. Then he which had received the one talent came and said, Lord, I knew thee that thou art an hard man, reaping where thou hast not sown, and gathering where thou hast not strawed:

25. And I was afraid, and went and hid thy talent in the earth: lo, there thou hast that is thine.

26. His lord answered and said unto him, Thou wicked and slothful servant, thou knewest that I reap where I sowed not, and gather where I have not strawed:

27. Thou oughtest therefore to have put my money to the exchangers, and then at my coming I should have received mine own with usury.

28. Take therefore the talent from him, and give it unto him, which hath ten talents.

29. For unto every one that hath shall be given, and he shall have abundance: but from him that hath not shall be taken away even that which he hath.

30. And cast ye the unprofitable servant into outer darkness: there shall be weeping and gnashing of teeth.
Matthew 25:14-30

Many folks who earnestly read this for the first time wonder if the Lord would really cast out an unprofitable servant?

Answer: Well, the answer is yes. That is exactly what happened in this parable. Remember the blessings and the curses.

First to understand the parable of the talents and Tuning into Heaven keep in mind that the Lord's kingdom is "to come." We are not now living in the kingdom of heaven. His kingdom is to come. As in the Lord's Prayer, "Thy kingdom come. Thy will be done in earth, as it is in heaven." The "Lord's Prayer" is in Matthew 6:9-13 and Luke 11:1-4

The "Lord's Prayer"

▶ 9. After this manner therefore pray ye: Our Father which art in heaven, Hallowed be thy name.

10. Thy kingdom come, Thy will be done in earth, as it is in heaven.

11. Give us this day our daily bread.

12. And forgive us our debts, as we forgive our debtors.

13. And lead us not into temptation, but deliver us from evil: For thine is the kingdom, and the power, and the glory, forever. Amen

Matthew: 6: 9-13

Keeping in mind that the Lord's Kingdom is not here now. But is to come: The parable of the talents starts out "For the kingdom of heaven is as a man travelling into a far country..." The "man" is also later referred to as their "lord" symbolizes our Lord. The "travelling into a far country" symbolizes our Lord coming into our world. "The far country" is this world. When the Lord returns He judges the servants. Their rewards and the Joy of the Lord are symbolic of Heaven.

"Tuning into Heaven" is going on here for the first two (2) servants. But the third servant appears to have fallen into false doctrine.

It further helps to comprehend this parable is that our own English word comes from this very parable of the Talents. "Talent" has the meaning capability/aptitude

Whereas here specifically "Talent" used in the parable was the term used for monetary currency like a dollar, dinero or peso. The talent was a quite large denomination of money.

Are you using your talents or hiding your talent?

The Lord does not give us an equal amount of talents. But He expects us to put our talent to use no matter what the amount of talents we receive. The two servants that put their talents to use received rewards "I will make thee ruler over many things: enter thou into the joy of thy lord." Wow! Being made a ruler and entering into the "Joy of the Lord." Heaven is being tuned in. The two servants receive blessings, prosperity and the Joy of the Lord.

Back now to the unprofitable servant who was cast out "into outer darkness: there shall be weeping and gnashing of teeth." Remember the blessings and the curses. We all have free will, the ability to make decisions, the ability to choose. He chose curses. Either wittingly or unwittingly he chose the curses.

Here is where "Truth Matters" comes into significance. The Creator God of the universe, the Higher Power gives or allows one to choose. The unprofitable servant hid his talent. He buried his talent believing in false doctrine.

Hiding one's talent apparently we should know by now is clearly contrary to Lord's will. How the third servant came about to believe this false doctrine is perplexing. The reasons he stated for believing that he should "hide his talent" appear phony not truthful.

If the servant really was so concerned that his Lord was a "hard man, reaping where thou hast not sown…" would not have the servant tried even a little to gain profit for the Lord to avert his wrath, like depositing the talent to gain interest?

How did this unprofitable servant really come about to make such a bad decision? We are not told if he ever reconsidered or had second thoughts. Somehow he fell under this false belief that he should not even try, never did, and he hid his talent until the Lord returned!

The Lord never said He punishes if one tries and fails.

The lord knew the servant's heart just as the Higher Power, the Creator God of the Universe, knows our hearts, since the heart is His jurisdiction. He knew the servant's heart. He knew the servant was a wicked and slothful servant who was unprofitable, which also means worthless.

CHAPTER 5
Truth

We need to hold in our hearts the Truth as the truth attracts the Blessings and the Joy of the Lord.

Jesus is the Truth. We hold the truth in our hearts: we hold Jesus in our hearts. Otherwise then just what are we holding in our hearts?
Answer: false doctrine, sin, evil, Satan. Holding false teachings in our hearts attracts curses.

Wow. This parable of the talents is intense. The implications! The unprofitable servant was cast out "into outer darkness: there shall be weeping and gnashing of teeth."

Remember the two (2) options when convicted? After Peter preached when they were convicted they chose the Lord. After Stephen preached when they were convicted they chose evil. Choose the Lord and His Way, not evil.

We choose to come to the Lord, we choose to follow the way of the Lord, the Higher Power, the Creator God, the God of the Universe, the Holy One, the Redeemer: The Lord who knows our hearts. We have a blessed assurance from Jesus that He shall not cast out any one that comes to Jesus, as Jesus promises:

▶ All that the Father giveth me shall come to me; and him that cometh to me I will in no wise cast out.

John 6:37

Further emphasizing this blessed assurance: All Christians are sinners. We struggle with sin. If needed go back and review the section on sin in the previous chapter.

The Lord knows our hearts. Everyone who looks to Jesus, believes in, delights in, trusts in and endeavors to rely upon Him, has His blessed assurance.

Jesus promises that He will not lose those that have been given to Him and believeth on Him will have eternal life: Note: seeth as used in "seeth the Son" means comprehend, know, like when someone says: "can you see what I am saying."

▶ 39. And this is the Father's will which hath sent me, that of all which he hath given me I should lose nothing, but should raise it up again at the last day.

40. And this is the will of him that sent me, that every one, which seeth the Son, and believeth on him, may have everlasting life: and I will raise him up at the last day.

John 6: 39-40

Next principal truths are presented and modern false doctrines are exposed. So hold on tightly because I am going to go through this material rapidly as it is only meant to be an exposure to the Truth and a repudiation of modern false teachings.

THE POWER OF MONEY IS IN SPENDING IT

Another pearl of wisdom that relates to the parable of the Talents is that the power of money is in spending it.

Money has no power when it is hidden in the ground. The power of money is released when a hospital is built, education is funded and food and shelter are provided. Otherwise, although money in hiding has a potential no one is getting any benefit of the power of the money because time is passing by and so are the lives of the people passing by.

Therefore, no benefit during that period of time the money is hidden. There is a loss because as time goes by quickly many opportunities for profit for the Lord, laying up treasures in Heaven, are lost after waiting too long. On account of inflation the value of money diminishes while hidden in the ground. Cash-in on the opportunity to be rich toward God!

The Parable of the Rich Man and the Plentiful Ground:

The parable of the rich man and the plentiful ground reveals not only that peoples' lives pass by which included the rich man's life passing by but likewise the opportunity to be rich toward God passes by as well:

▶ 16. And he spake a parable unto them, saying, The ground of a certain rich man brought forth plentifully:

17. And he thought within himself, saying, What shall I do, because I have no room where to bestow my fruits?

18. And he said, This will I do: I will pull down my barns, and build greater; and there will I bestow all my fruits and my goods.

19. And I will say to my soul, Soul, thou hast much goods laid up for many years; take thine ease, eat, drink, and be merry.

20. But God said unto him, Thou fool, this night thy soul shall be required of thee: then whose shall those things be, which thou hast provided?

21. So is he that layeth up treasure for himself, and is not rich toward God.

Luke 12:16-21

Jesus explains to the Disciples that where your treasures are then there is where your heart is. Not to accumulate wealth for one's self. Use your resources to be rich toward God. Then "all these things (Blessings) shall be added unto you":

▶ 31. But rather seek ye the kingdom of God; and all these things shall be added unto you.

32. ... 33. ... a treasure in the heavens that faileth not, where no thief approacheth, neither moth corrupteth.

34. For where your treasure is, there will your heart be also.

Luke 12:31-34

Prelude\Forward, Truth: Sabbath, Saturday or Sunday?

The Lord never changes. He is consistent.
Man changes. Man is inconsistent:

The Higher Spirit, the Good Heavenly Father, the Holy One, the Creator, the Protector, God Almighty the Redeemer, He is never changing.

▶ For I am the LORD, I change not; therefore ye sons of Jacob are not consumed.

Malachi 3:6

▶ 8 Jesus Christ the same yesterday, and to day, and for ever.

Hebrews 13:8

Our Lord is abundantly willing to make clear to His heirs (us), His immutability (unchanging) nature, His Counsel, (guidance, direction and warning), He confirmed it with an oath.
Note: Immutability means unchangeable.
Note: Counsel means guidance, direction and warning.

▶ 17. Wherein God, willing more abundantly to shew unto the heirs of promise the immutability of his counsel, confirmed it by an oath:

18. That by two immutable things, in which it was impossible for God to lie, we might have a strong consolation, who have fled for refuge to lay hold upon the hope set before us:

19. Which hope we have as an anchor of the soul, both sure and stedfast, and which entereth into that within the veil;

Hebrews 6:17-19

The Lord never changes, therefore the Lord cannot lie.

▶ God is not a man, that he should lie; neither the son of man, that he should repent: hath he said, and shall he not do it? or hath he spoken, and shall he not make it good?

Numbers 23:19

The Lord never changes, therefore the Lord cannot lie.
A lie by the Lord is impossible given that the Lord's counsel, that is His guidance, direction and warning are always exactly the same. No change whatsoever then no possibility of a lie.

Man changes and is inconsistent. Man lies and makes errors.

Jesus is the Truth. We hold the truth in our hearts: we hold Jesus in our hearts. Otherwise holding false teachings in our hearts attracts curses, sin, evil, Satan into our heart.

In the parable of the Talents the unprofitable servant was cast out "into outer darkness: there shall be weeping and gnashing of teeth." Remember the blessings and the curses. We all have free will, the ability to make decisions, the ability to choose. He chose the curses. Either wittingly or unwittingly he chose the curses.

▶ All scripture is given by inspiration of God, and is profitable for doctrine, for reproof, for correction, for instruction in righteousness:

2 Timothy 3:16

Choose these precepts of the Bible, Tune-In Heaven and enter into the Blessings, the Joy and the Protection of the Lord, the Higher Spirit, the Good Heavenly Father, the Holy One who is the Creator of the Universe, the Redeemer.

THE SABBATH: SATURDAY OR SUNDAY

What day did the Creator God of the Universe, the Higher
Power, the Holy One bless and sanctify?
Answer: The Seventh Day Sabbath, which is Saturday.

▶ And God blessed the seventh day, and sanctified it:
because that in it he had rested from all his work which God
created and made.

Genesis 2:3

Is there further Biblical authority of the Sabbath?

Answer: Yes, abundantly yes. Key Biblical Precept:

The Sabbath is Number 4 of the Ten Commandments given
by God Almighty, the Higher Power, the Holy One:

▶ 8. Remember the Sabbath day, to keep it holy.

9. Six days shalt thou labour, and do all thy work:

10. But the seventh day is the Sabbath of the Lord thy God: in
it thou shalt not do any work, thou, nor thy son, nor thy
daughter, thy manservant, nor thy maidservant, nor thy cattle,
nor thy stranger that is within thy gates:

11. For in six days the Lord made heaven and earth, the sea, and
all that in them is, and rested the seventh day: wherefore the
Lord blessed the Sabbath day, and hallowed it.

Exodus 4: 8-11

What are the actions suppose to be on the Sabbath?

Answer: Rest

Note: Convocation "formal assembly of the people together"

► Six days shall work be done: but the seventh day is the Sabbath of rest, a holy convocation; ye shall do no work therein: it is the Sabbath of the Lord in all your dwellings.

Leviticus 23:3

What would be a sign between the creator God of the universe, the Higher Power, the Redeemer and me so I would know that the Lord is my God?

Answer: The Lord Hallowed, Sanctified, made "Holy" the Sabbath, we then keep "Honor" the Sabbath:

► 19. I am the Lord your God; walk in my statutes, and keep my judgments, and do them;

20. And hallow my Sabbaths; and they shall be a sign between me and you, that ye may know that I am the Lord your God. (Note: Hallow means "Honor\Make as Holy")

Ezekiel 20:19-20

Is there specific Biblical support that the Creator God of the Universe, the Higher Power, the Holy One will reward my obedience of the Sabbath with Blessings?

Answer: Yes, in Isaiah:

► 13. If thou turn away thy foot from the Sabbath, from doing thy pleasure on my holy day; and call the Sabbath a delight, the holy of the Lord, honourable; and shalt honour him, not doing thine own ways, nor finding thine own pleasure, nor speaking thine own words:

14. Then shalt thou delight thyself in the Lord; and I will cause thee to ride upon the high places of the earth, and feed thee with the heritage of Jacob thy father: for the mouth of the Lord hath spoken it.

Isaiah 58: 13-14

What about Sunday?

Now many good folks who are experiencing this for the first time may be surprised and or thinking what about "Sunday." How did Sunday, the first day of the week become the Sabbath? Did Jesus change the Sabbath to Sunday?

Answer: No Jesus did not change the Sabbath to Sunday:

▶ 17. Think not that I am come to destroy the law, or the prophets: I am not come to destroy, but to fulfil.

18. For verily I say unto you, Till heaven and earth pass, one jot or one tittle shall in no wise pass from the law, till all be fulfilled.

19. Whosoever therefore shall break one of these least commandments, and shall teach men so, he shall be called the least in the kingdom of heaven: but whosoever shall do and teach them, the same shall be called great in the kingdom of heaven.

Matthew 5:17-19

All through out the New Testament are accounts of Jesus keeping, teaching and performing miracles on the Sabbath, He did not change the Sabbath to Sunday, No Way:

▶ And he came to Nazareth, where he had been brought up: and, as his custom was, he went into the synagogue on the Sabbath day, and stood up for to read.

Luke 4:16

Jesus was the "Lord of the Sabbath." He would have told us if He had changed the Sabbath.

▶ Therefore the Son of man is Lord also of the Sabbath. Mark 2:28

Jesus never said anything of the sort about changing the Sabbath from Saturday to Sunday.

What about the apostles, those who witnessed Jesus, did they report that Jesus changed the Sabbath from Saturday to Sunday?

Answer: No, the Apostles never said or wrote anything about Jesus changing the Sabbath from Saturday to Sunday.

Apostles, Background:

After Christ completed His ministry, died on the cross and resurrected, the apostles carried out the mission of Jesus: to preach the good news of Jesus Christ. Known as the Great Commission.

▶ 18. And Jesus came and spake unto them, saying, All power is given unto me in heaven and in earth.

19. Go ye therefore, and teach all nations, baptizing them in the name of the Father, and of the Son, and of the Holy Ghost:

20. Teaching them to observe all things whatsoever I have commanded you: and, lo, I am with you always, even unto the end of the world. Amen.

Matthew 28:18-20

CHAPTER 5
Truth

Luke made record of the Acts of the Apostles, known as Acts in the Bible, wherein, Apostle Paul himself when he was in Corinth taught in the synagogue every Sabbath:

▶ And he reasoned in the synagogue every Sabbath, and persuaded the Jews and the Greeks.
Acts 18:4

Apostle Paul in his letter to the Hebrews, confirms the seventh day Saturday, as the Sabbath:

▶ 4. For he spake in a certain place of the seventh day on this wise, And God did rest the seventh day from all his works.
5. And in this place again, If they shall enter into my rest.
6. Seeing therefore it remaineth that some must enter therein, and they to whom it was first preached entered not in because of unbelief:
7. Again, he limiteth a certain day, saying in David, To day, after so long a time; as it is said, To day if ye will hear his voice, harden not your hearts.
8. For if Jesus had given them rest, then would he not afterward have spoken of another day.
9. There remaineth therefore a rest to the people of God.
10. For he that is entered into his rest, he also hath ceased from his own works, as God did from his.
11. Let us labour therefore to enter into that rest, lest any man fall after the same example of unbelief.
Hebrews 4: 4-11

The Apostles never made the switch to Sunday. Neither did the Apostles write anything about Jesus changing the Sabbath from Saturday to Sunday. Nothing like that ever happened!

TRUTH:
YOU ONLY RECEIVE SABBATH BLESSINGS
FOR OBSERVING THE SEVENTH DAY SABBATH:

You cannot benefit from false doctrine:

You can only benefit from knowing the truth.
Truth is wholly worthy:

You only receive the Blessings of observing the Sabbath on the seventh day, Sabbath, which is Saturday.

The seventh day Sabbath: That is the day that Father, God blessed and Hallowed (Sanctified), the seventh day, Sabbath.

You cannot receive the Sabbath Blessing of observing the Sabbath if you observe Sunday, it is a different day, it is the first day of the week!

The Lord delights in all our prayers and worship regardless of the day. But you cannot receive the Sabbath Blessings of the Sabbath if on the Sabbath, which is actually Saturday, you work and ignore the fact that it is the Sabbath.

Jesus really would have told us if He had changed the Sabbath. He did not change it.

How then did the Sabbath get changed from Saturday, the seventh day of the week to Sunday the first day of the week?

Answer: Changed by Man.

Man changed the Sabbath from the seventh day of the week to Sunday the first day of the week.

HISTORY:

- Emperor Constantine I, the Roman Emperor who legalized Christianity made the first Sunday law in order to unite the Pagans (sun worshippers) and the Christians in 321 A.D.

- The Sunday law was officially confirmed by the Council of Laodicea in 364 A.D.

- Pope Leo XIII, pope from 1878 until 1903, one of the most forceful popes of the nineteenth century, explained that Popes have such authority, and also many known higher-up Catholics in their writings teach that the Pope has the power, and, then some mock the Protestants for following the Sunday Law because the Protestants are not following the Biblical precepts but are following the precepts of man.

WARNING: As you reflect on the Sabbath Truth:
Do not share unless you are absolutely positive. Otherwise you may be humiliated and hurt. The warning from Jesus:
Note: Rend means to separate or tear into parts.

▶ Give not that which is holy unto the dogs, neither cast ye your pearls before swine, lest they trample them under their feet, and turn again and rend you.
Matthew 7:6

Not everyone will have encouraging words for the new believer. There are ones who will "rend" the new believer.

Find delight in the Sabbath. Rest on the Sabbath. Delight in the Sabbath.

In Genesis the Lord sanctified and blessed the Sabbath. Sanctify means make Holy, dedicated to God, purified free from sin. You can enter into the rest with the Higher Power, the Creator God of the Universe, the Holy One, and enter into His Joy, and receive the Blessings of the Lord. This is real. This is the Truth. You may be asking: What should I do now?

Answer: Keep the Sabbath day as the Lord commanded:

▶ 12. Keep the Sabbath day to sanctify it, as the Lord thy God hath commanded thee.

13. Six days thou shalt labour, and do all thy work:

14. But the seventh day is the Sabbath of the Lord thy God: in it thou shalt not do any work, thou, nor thy son, nor thy daughter, nor thy manservant, nor thy maidservant, nor thine ox, nor thine ass, nor any of thy cattle, nor thy stranger that is within thy gates; that thy manservant and thy maidservant may rest as well as thou.

15. And remember that thou wast a servant in the land of Egypt, and that the Lord thy God brought thee out thence through a mighty hand and by a stretched out arm: therefore the Lord thy God commanded thee to keep the Sabbath day.

Deuteronomy 5:12-15

WHEN YOU ARE DEAD YOU ARE DEAD: RESURRECTION OR SPIRITUALISM

There are no ghosts, no spirits lingering around between our world and the next. The dead are dead.

The Lord and His Angels come and go into this world from Heaven. The Lord's angels and the Higher Power, the Creator God of the Universe, the Holy One, enters between these two realms at the will of the Lord.

Satan and his demons were cast down to this world and hence are restricted to this world.

The Bible is very clear about what happens to anyone when they die. The dead are dead:

▶ For the living know that they shall die: but the dead know not any thing, neither have they any more a reward; for the memory of them is forgotten.

Ecclesiastes 9:5

▶ His breath goeth forth, he returneth to his earth; in that very day his thoughts perish.

Psalms 146:4

▶ Thou hidest thy face, they are troubled: thou takest away their breath, they die, and return to their dust.

Psalms 104:29

▶ So man lieth down, and riseth not: till the heavens be no more, they shall not awake, nor be raised out of their sleep.

Job 14:12

Jesus resurrected on the third day. The tomb was empty. The Resurrected Jesus appeared for forty (40) days and was witnessed by many performing infallible proofs.

The Bible teaches the Resurrection: the Dead in Christ will be Resurrected.
When Jesus returns to the earth: That is the second coming of the Lord Jesus, the dead in Christ will be resurrected up to meet the Lord in the sky and those in Christ who are still alive will be called up, transformed and will meet the Lord in the sky. This is the promise of Jesus!

There is nothing in the Bible that teaches that when we die we immediately go to heaven. Jesus believed and taught the resurrection, Jesus resurrected and then after the ascension of Jesus to Heaven the apostles taught the resurrection. So then thereafter the early church taught the resurrection.

The false teaching of Spiritualism conflicts with the Biblical resurrection. Spiritualism is contrary to the Bible precepts.

Spiritualism:
Spiritualism is the false concept that a spiritual realm or universe overshadows the material world: Spiritualism falsely teaches when one dies then one crosses over into this spiritual realm or universe. This is not so!

Spiritualism was popularized in 1847 through 1848 after the "Fox Sisters" 15-year-old Margaret Fox and her 11-old sister Kay Fox became a sensation.

It started when the girls frightened their superstitious mother by creating sounds that echoed through their farmhouse at night in New York by popping or cracking their toe knuckles like one would snap their fingers.

Rumors that the "Fox House" was haunted spread far and wide. The girls became popular making deceptively noises when contacting ghosts and in that time and afterwards spiritualism increased.

There is no logic to a reality of a future resurrection ever taking place if everyone has already "crossed over" at death. There would be no one to even be resurrected. They would already be somewhere else – the spiritual realm?
It makes no sense!

The Bible makes it abundantly clear that the resurrection is true. Most folks will recognize this Biblical verse:

▶ 15. That whosoever believeth in him should not perish, but have eternal life.

16. For God so loved the world, that he gave his only begotten Son, that whosoever believeth in him should not perish, but have everlasting life.

17. For God sent not his Son into the world to condemn the world; but that the world through him might be saved.

John 3:15-17

Let us start with the passage "That whosoever believeth in him should not perish..." In error some interpret "perish" to mean death. But think about it: Did not anyone die in Jesus day? Yes, of course people died in the days of Jesus as Jesus Himself died on the cross at Calvary. Christians do not avoid dying who believe in Jesus. People have been dying since before and after the days of Christ.

So then if Jesus did not mean that you will not die if you believe in Jesus then just what did He mean with "you would not perish?"

Answer: Jesus was talking about the resurrection. When Jesus returns to earth that is the second coming of Jesus, the dead in Christ and those alive in Christ are called up to meet Jesus in the air - then you will not perish but have everlasting life.

► 16. For the Lord himself shall descend from heaven with a shout, with the voice of the archangel, and with the trump of God: and the dead in Christ shall rise first:

17. Then we which are alive and remain shall be caught up together with them in the clouds, to meet the Lord in the air: and so shall we ever be with the Lord.

1 Thessalonians 4:16-17

► Neither can they die any more: for they are equal unto the angels; and are the children of God, being the children of the resurrection.

Luke 20: 36

What about the wicked at the Second Coming of Jesus?
Answer: At the second coming of Jesus the wicked will be destroyed "with the brightness of his coming."

► And then shall that wicked be revealed, whom the Lord shall consume with the spirit of his mouth, and shall destroy with the brightness of his coming:

2 Thessalonians 2:8

There is no burning in hell for an eternity. The wicked will be destroyed forever "with everlasting destruction." Thereafter, the wicked cannot ever be restored back to life.

► 7. And to you who are troubled rest with us, when the Lord Jesus shall be revealed from heaven with his mighty angels,

8. In flaming fire taking vengeance on them that know not God, and that obey not the gospel of our Lord Jesus Christ:

9. Who shall be punished with everlasting destruction from the presence of the Lord, and from the glory of his power.

2 Thessalonians 1:7-9

"Already With"
the Lord, the Creator of the Universe, the Higher Spirit:

There are at least three human beings, including: Enoch, Elijah and Moses "Already With" the Higher Spirit, The Holy One, dwelling in Heaven that is occupied by the Lord, the Creator of the Universe, and His Heavenly Host of Angels.

Enoch:

▶ "And Enoch walked with God: and he was not; for God took him"
Genesis 5:24

Elijah:

▶ And it came to pass, as they still went on, and talked, that, behold, there appeared a chariot of fire, and horses of fire, and parted them both asunder; and Elijah went up by a whirlwind into heaven.
2 Kings 2:13

Moses:

▶ Yet Michael the archangel, when contending with the devil he disputed about the body of Moses, durst not bring against him a railing accusation, but said, The Lord rebuke thee.
Jude: 1:9

Now of course there could be a number more of people that are already with the Lord in heaven. Plainly though the way of these three and maybe some more others way to Heaven is not the representative way to Heaven. The resurrection is the way that the majority of us in Christ will go to Heaven.

Near Death Experiences:

Everyone today has heard accounts of near death experiences. Are they real? Answer: Yes.

Now the first thing to consider is that those who had these near death experiences did not die, the experience was a near death experience but they did not die since, obviously they would not be here to give us the account.
Nevertheless most clearly did connect into the heavenly realm. I dare here now to call this a portal, a passageway to Heaven. Angels absolutely come in an out of this world.
So apparently there are portals between here and Heaven.
This relates to the theme that we can Tune-In Heaven.
We do not need to come close to death to experience a touch of heaven. The Lord, the Creator God, the Higher Spirit, the Holy One has his arms stretched out now for us to enter into His Joy and receive His Blessings. We need give thanks and obey His commandments to Tune-In Heaven.

Heaven and Earth Portal:

Is there any Biblical support for a "Portal?" Yes, in Genesis, Jacob had a dream or a vision of a "Ladder" with angels ascending and descending between Heaven and earth. He awakes and realizes the "Ladder" is the gate to Heaven.

▶ 12. And he dreamed, and behold a ladder set up on the earth, and the top of it reached to heaven: and behold the angels of God ascending and descending on it.

13. And, behold, the Lord stood above it, and said, I am the Lord God of Abraham thy father, and the God of Isaac: the land whereon thou liest, to thee will I give it, and to thy seed;

Genesis 28:12-13

▶ … this is none other but the house of God, and this is the gate of heaven.
Genesis 28:17

Jacob had a dream or a vision of a "Ladder" with angels ascending and descending between Heaven and earth. He awakes and realizes the "Ladder" is the gate to Heaven.

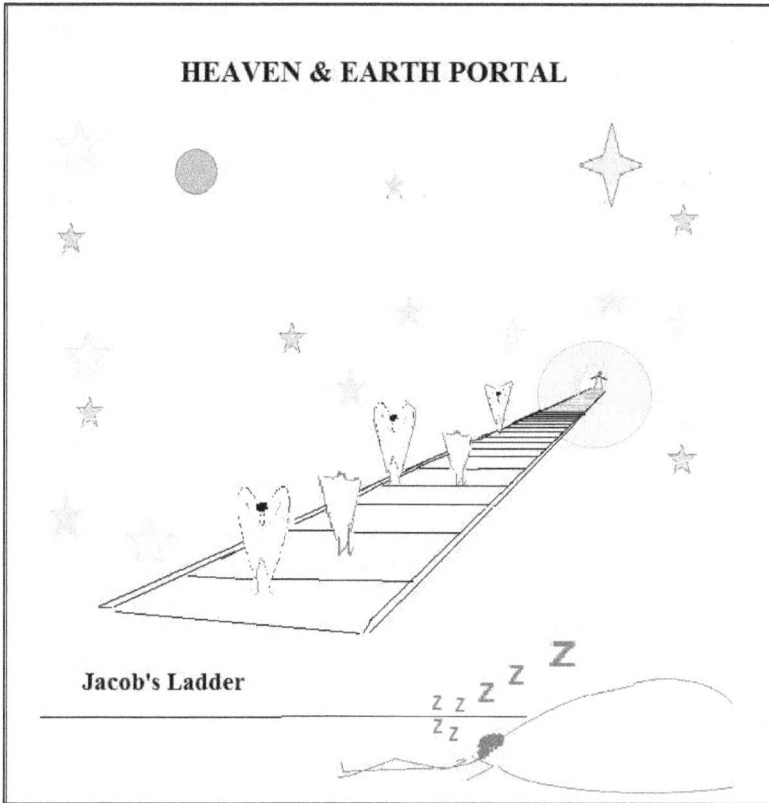

HEAVEN & EARTH PORTAL

Jacob's Ladder

The Angels come and go from Heaven to earth, but what about the demons?

Answer: Satan and the evil sprits were cast down from Heaven to the earth, and are restricted to earth. At the end of times Satan and the evil sprits will be judged and destroyed.

Jesus explained how Satan and the evil spirits were cast down from Heaven to earth while instructing the "Seventy Two." Jesus in addition to the twelve disciples had appointed "Seventy Two." Jesus sent them out ahead of Him to heal the sick. The Seventy Two returned full of joy declaring that even the evil spirits (devils) had to obey Your Name (Jesus.)

▶ And the Seventy Two returned again with joy, saying, Lord, even the devils are subject unto us through thy name.

Luke 10: 17

Jesus explains that Satan fell from heaven:

▶ And he said unto them, I beheld Satan as lightning fall from heaven.

Luke 10: 18

The demons (Satan's angels) were cast down with Satan:

▶ And the great dragon was cast out, that old serpent, called the Devil, and Satan, which deceiveth the whole world: he was cast out into the earth, and his angels were cast out with him.

Revelation 12:9

CHAPTER 5
Truth

In summary:

Here on this earth the Angles of the Lord, come and go from Heaven to earth according to the Will of the Creator of the Universe, the Higher Spirit, The Holy One.

Then in regards to Satan and his followers the evil spirits they have been cast down to earth and their access to heaven is blocked. In the end of times Satan and these wicked tormenting demons will be judged and utterly destroyed forever by the Just and Holy, God Almighty.

SUPERNATURAL EXPERIENCES THAT ARE NATURAL EXPERIENCES:

Next what about supernatural experiences? Such as people thinking of someone then that someone telephones. A mother knows her child is in danger or hurting and then finds out that her child is in fact, actually in danger or hurting. You "feel someone looking at you" and then you look and see that someone who is actually looking at you.

Rupert Sheldrake, Author of Morphic Resonance:
 < subject, recognized authority>

There is another explanation for these supernatural experiences offered by the renowned Biologist, Rupert Sheldrake that he has named Morphic Resonance.
Top quality material, is readily available on his Website, the Internet and in Bookstores.

Morphic Resonance is being outlined here, not being fully developed. Do not get bogged down. Keep reading Tune-In Heaven. For many, you may only need to know the sound, scientific outline presented here. Others are encouraged to read the works of Rupert Sheldrake for an in-depth understanding of Morphic Resonance keeping in mind always to sort out any doctrine not consistent with the Bible.

Many human experiences that are labeled "supernatural" are not supernatural experiences at all, but are natural experiences. These experiences can be explained by Morphic Fields (sometimes referred to as morph fields.)

Morphic Fields are conceptually like gravitational or magnetic fields. There are numerous Morphic Fields, and even nested morph fields within morph fields. Morphic Fields are the medium, where real-time communication between members takes place and is also like a reservoir where stored information, including past and present member experiences is available to individual members of their specific group. Groups are such as giraffes, people, families, fish, trout, salmon, plants and minerals for example.

It would seem that individual members would have some sort of right to use, access, key that would allow only members access to the morph fields and restrict others from entering the morph field. Otherwise predators such as bears and wild cats would have access to the morph fields of their prey.

Also there are forming and organizing biological Morphic Fields that provide developmental genetic instructions.

The information stored in these Morphic Fields is like information stored on a hard drive of a computer. Our brain is like an antenna that connects, receives and communicates by way of resonance within Morphic Fields. The closer the relationships then the more likely the connection or communication within the Morphic Fields.

Rupert Sheldrake postulates that Morphic Fields explain the precision swimming of schools of fish and the accurate formations of flying flocks of birds. Fish or birds could hardly adjust their individual swimming or flight by seeing the surrounding fish or birds moving around them without one of them bumping into one another. The flocks of migratory birds fly and schools of fish swim with such precision that it is a joy to experience.

I found in the Bible several extraordinary experiences of communicating or connecting of this world with the Lord or His heavenly kingdom. In Genesis, the "blood cries from the ground" to the Lord:

After Cane slew Able:

▶ And he said, What hast thou done? the voice of thy brother's blood crieth unto me from the ground.

Genesis 4:10

The Prophet Isaiah:

▶ For ye shall go out with joy, and be led forth with peace: the mountains and the hills shall break forth before you into singing, and all the trees of the field shall clap their hands.

Isaiah 55:12

No Space Aliens or Inter-dimensional Beings.

There are no outer-space aliens, no inter-dimensional alien beings only angels and demons.

If aliens came to this planet it would be like the English, Spanish or French when they came to the New World, that is North America and South America.

The aliens would walk or move (however they would move about), freely wherever they wanted to go. They would go in broad daylight or night without hiding themselves. Just like you or me would go through the park. Are you afraid of a squirrel or any bird attacking? No. We know we are superior to all animals. They are not a threat. Well then, how about an alien that has the super intelligence and super technology to get here - really be like?

Answer: No hiding aliens.

Any such alien explorers would be in plain view. The alien of course would be prepared with some sort of protective force field and/or defensive weapon to stun or eliminate attackers. Hiding in the darkness, misty or disguised appearances and mimicking the dead are the traits of evil sprits or demons.

Apostle Paul describes a Christian friend that had an experience that today one might misunderstand as an inter-dimensional alien encounter but Apostle Paul understands that his friend "was caught up into paradise:"

▶ 2. I knew a man in Christ above fourteen years ago, whether in the body, I cannot tell; or whether out of the body, I cannot tell: God knoweth; such an one caught up to the third heaven.

3. And I knew such a man, whether in the body, or out of the body, I cannot tell: God knoweth;

4. How that he was caught up into paradise, and heard unspeakable words, which it is not lawful for a man to utter.

2 Corinthians 12: 2-4

I would be remiss not to give a further example of a heavenly encounter that could today be misunderstood as an alien encounter in referring to the experience of Apostle John being "in the Spirit" as described in the Revelation of Apostle John:

▶ 10. I was in the Spirit on the Lord's day, and heard behind me a great voice, as of a trumpet,

11. Saying, I am Alpha and Omega, the first and the last: and, What thou seest, write in a book, and send it unto the seven churches which are in Asia; unto Ephesus, and unto Smyrna, and unto Pergamos, and unto Thyatira, and unto Sardis, and unto Philadelphia, and unto Laodicea.

12. And I turned to see the voice that spake with me. And being turned, I saw seven golden candlesticks;

13. And in the midst of the seven candlesticks one like unto the Son of man, clothed with a garment down to the foot, and girt about the paps with a golden girdle.

14. His head and his hairs were white like wool, as white as snow; and his eyes were as a flame of fire;

15. And his feet like unto fine brass, as if they burned in a furnace; and his voice as the sound of many waters.

Revelation 1:10-15

OUR HOPE IS IN THE RESURRECTION:

Our hope is in the resurrection as Apostle Paul explains:

▶ 12. Now if Christ be preached that he rose from the dead, how say some among you that there is no resurrection of the dead?

13. But if there be no resurrection of the dead, then is Christ not risen:

14. And if Christ be not risen, then is our preaching vain, and your faith is also vain.

15. Yea, and we are found false witnesses of God; because we have testified of God that he raised up Christ: whom he raised not up, if so be that the dead rise not.

16. For if the dead rise not, then is not Christ raised:

17. And if Christ be not raised, your faith is vain; ye are yet in your sins.

18. Then they also which are fallen asleep in Christ are perished.

19. If in this life only we have hope in Christ, we are of all men most miserable.

CHAPTER 5
Truth

20. But now is Christ risen from the dead, and become the firstfruits of them that slept.

1 Corinthians 15: 12-20

Prelude\Forward to Creation and Noah's Flood.

Next, Biblical scientific truths from antiquity to present day are contrasted to modern false doctrines in order to familiarize folks with the counter-arguments against these modern false doctrines.

Many folks have never heard of scientific Biblical Truths or any Defense to Biblical Truths. Mainstream news media only discusses modern false doctrines. Christian theories are dismissed as foolishness, as idiotic beliefs of the uneducated ignoramus. They resort to name calling because they have no answers! We do not name call them back.

Truths and modern false doctrines are being outlined here, not being fully developed. Do not get bogged down. Keep reading Tune-In Heaven. For many, you may only need to know that there are sound, scientific answers that are supported in the Bible.

On the other hand, many of you are already familiar with some or most of these upcoming Christian scientific concepts being presented or you quickly "get it" if so, just skip through to the next concept.

The proof of Creation and Noah's Flood that exists outside of this book is truly a voluminous amount of top quality material, readily available on the Internet and in Bookstores.

The upcoming Biblical scientific Truths along with pearls of wisdom that are outlined here within are truly life changing, transforming precepts to Tune-In to Heaven.

NOAH'S FLOOD:
NOAH'S FLOOD, GLOBAL EVENT OR
GEOLOGICAL, LOCAL EVENTS & GRADUALISM

Jesus, the disciples, Moses, the prophets, believed in the flood.

Moses is this author of the first five books of the Bible, inspired by the Lord. Genesis includes the account of the Flood, so then Moses, who wrote Genesis, inspired by God, believed in the Flood. The prophets of the Old Testament believed in the Flood. Additionally there are plenty of non-Biblical historical accounts of the flood:

Josephus:

Flavius Josephus, a renowned first-century Roman-Jewish scholar and historian believed in the Flood and quoted other such early scholars including quoting Berosus the Chaldean: "It is said that there is still some part of this ship in Armenia, at the mountain of the Cordyeans; and that some people carry off pieces of the bitumen, which they take away, and use chiefly as amulets (good luck charm) for the averting mischief."

Josephus also refers to Nicolaus of Damascus, born in 40 BC, who was a predecessor of Josephus. Nicolaus was an intimate friend of Herod the Great, and was the tutor of the children of Mark Antony and Cleopatra. Josephus quoting Nicolaus: "There is a great mountain in Armenia, over Minyas, called Baris, upon which it is reported that many who fled at the time of the Deluge were saved; and that one who was carried in an ark came on shore upon the top of it; and that the remains of the timber were a great while preserved. This might be the man about whom Moses the legislator of the Jews wrote."

Also Josephus refers to Hieronymus the Egyptian and Mnaseas as making the same reports. The works of Josephus have survived and are presently readily available for purchase. But unfortunately most of these other ancient manuscripts referenced by Josephus were destroyed, are lost or only fragments remain.

The Ancient Book of Jasher:

The Ancient Book of Jasher is a historical record of antiquity written by ancient Jews, published in 1840 by MM Noah & AS Gould, includes an extensive account of the Flood and Pre-Flood up to through the time of Joshua. This book is presently available for purchase.

Classical Scientists:

In the 17th and 18th centuries the accepted geological explanation for sedimentary rock and their fossilized content was Noah's Flood.

Nicolas Steno, the leading authority, since the 17th century of geology rock layers, layering study of sedimentary and layered volcanic rocks, which is still being taught today, advocated Noah's Flood.

Sir Isaac Newton's hand-picked successor at Cambridge, John Woodward, whose studies on the sedimentary processes established the foundation for the modern day study of sediments and the processes that result in their formation and the scientific study of topographic, both advocated Noah's Flood.

Henry M. Morris, Creationist < subject, recognized authority>:

Modern day, Henry M. Morris "the Father of Creation Science" one of the founders of the renowned: Creation Research Society and the Institute for Creation Research.

Propounded Noah's Flood, served as a professor at the University of Louisiana at Lafayette and at Southern Illinois University in 1957 and Virginia Polytechnic Institute and State University (Virginia Tech) In 1959.

October 6, 1918 – February 25, 2006.

Institute for Creation Research is a source of proof of Creation and Noah's Flood: Top quality material, readily available on the Institute for Creation Research (ICR) Website, the Internet and in Bookstores.

Questions:

So then what happened then that academic teachings turned to denying the Flood, denying that the earth experienced a global catastrophic event referred to throughout history as "Noah's Flood" or the "Deluge?" Who exactly came up with this phony idea that the Flood had no part in shaping the earth in the past because there was no Flood?

Who came up with the idea that the climate and the same geological events occurring today are the same events that occurred in the past and only these same past and present geological events shaped the earth in the past?

Answer: Charles Lyell

Charles Lyell, an English attorney, author of Principles of Geology, first published in 3 volumes in 1830–1833, he invented the "Geological Column" out of theory, not supported by any physical facts, no geological discoveries.

Nowhere can you actually find the arrangement of layers in the earth as taught by the Geological Column, still being taught today. Fact: Nowhere does the sequence of these layers exist on earth as described in Charles Lyell's geological column!

The phony theory is that earth's surface changes are caused by climate and geological events that occurred in the past that are just the same climate and geological events that occur today. Deniers of the global Flood.

The supporting explanation for this lame theory called "Gradualism," which is totally false is that you can see that there are layers in the earth. Therefore because there are layers in the earth that proves the events that occurred in the past are just the same as today. This explanation is mere speculation. Then he claims the layers supposedly form a record of the climate and geological events of the past such as earthquakes, local floods and hurricanes. The worldwide Noah's Flood is denied. Although the gradualism theory is riddled with contradicting physical evidence it is still being taught in the classrooms today.

Yes there is contradicting physical evidence to gradualism. The evidence is that the earth's layers were formed rapidly not gradually.

How can the phony gradualism theory be exposed?

Answer: To expose this phony gradualism theory as a "scientific attack" on true history and on the Lord the question is asked: what would the earth look like if Noah's Flood is true and what would we expect to find?

The answer is that the earth would look exactly just like it does with mountains, oceans and plains. If you fly across the continental United States, when you are at approximately, 30,000 foot altitude over the western U.S. then what you see out the jet window is the many great canyons appearing as "erosion ditches" over the great western plains where the water drained down off of the continent into the Gulf of Mexico. I personally have viewed this. It is awesome evidence of the Flood of God almighty!

What about the rock layers? What do we see?

Answer: We see a sedimentary layer of rock that covers the entire earth. Sediment is deposited by water There is a sedimentary layer of rock that covers the entire earth. If the world experienced a global flood a sedimentary layer of rock would cover the entire earth. Also it would be full of fossils. And, that is exactly what you would expect the geologist to find. And find they did.

There is no other conceivable explanation for the sedimentary layer covering the entire earth other the Noah's Flood. Their opposing theory is too convoluted, imaginative and just fabricated, which simply was invented for the purpose to deny God. And, there is no denying the sedimentary layer of rock that covers the entire earth because yes it is everywhere!

Dr Steve Austin, Creationist. **< subject, recognized authority>**

Dr Steve Austin, the foremost authority of Mount Saint Helens.

Top quality material, readily available on his Website, the Internet and in Bookstores.

Fly over video and photography of layers forming rapidly were obtained at Mount Saint Helens during the 1980 volcano eruption that evidences actual quickly occurring rock layers. There are actual pictures and videos that show the quickly occurring rock layers during and following the Mount Saint Helens volcano eruption.

The prominent rock layer features visible at the Grand Canyon, Yellowstone, and other places occurred rapidly. Even though "gradualism" is clearly disproved by evidence, this theory that rock layers have taken millions of years to occur is still being taught. The earth's rock layers actually occurred quickly during the catastrophic events that occurred in and after Noah's Flood such as the volcano eruptions, the deluge of rainwater and the receding floodwater.

If you drive across Pennsylvania on the turnpike or on an interstate highway that passes through mountains you can see the layers in the rock as you ride by them. The layers go one-way and then another way, as they are often not even horizontal. These layers did not build up over millions of years they were laid down rapidly during Noah's Flood. Also keep in mind that the layers are not in the sequence of the geological column. Nowhere on earth are the layers in the sequence of the geological column!

Ice Core "Layer" Dating Discredited, Disproved and Invalidated:

In July 1942, participating in Operation Bolero, World War 2 (WW2), six (6) American planes two (2) B-17 bombers and six (6) P-38 fighters went down in the cold snow and ice in Greenland. All of the 25 crewmembers were unharmed and rescued by dogsled. Because of the severe weather conditions the planes could not be recovered and were abandoned. Now known as the "Lost Squadron."

Beginning in 1988/1990 the Lost Squadron was discovered and located buried under 263 feet of ice. The planes were only there about forty-eight (48) years. But the Ice core layer exceeded 135,000 annual layers.

Question: So if the planes were there for less that fifty (50) years then what does that say about the ice core layer theory that ages the planes at about 135,000 years?

Answer: Ice Core Layer theory is discredited, disproved and invalidated.

Locals report that every storm produces one of these wafer-thin layers and that there is one storm after another in this severe weather area. These layers of ice are not annual layers! Multiple layers are formed within days! Also discredited is the theory that the Antarctic was formed 160,000 years ago that is based on this discredited ice layer theory.

Question: What would happen to all the vegetation that was soaked in water, destroyed and buried in the Flood?

Answer: One would expect to find large underground reservoirs of petroleum, produced from the compressed decayed vegetation. Yes of course that is what we find, large vast underground reservoirs of petroleum.

How about fossils?

We would expect to find large numbers of fossils clustered together because the receding Floodwaters would have caused the high number of animals destroyed in the Flood to gather together and accumulated in an area.

Then as the Floodwaters drained off, then if there were minerals in the water then fossilization would occur. Many of these fossil graveyards have been found.

The Flood deniers used to call them tar pits. The lame explanation was that animals like lions, elephants and dinosaurs fell into a tar pit got stuck and met their demise. Also we would expect to find fossils in the sedimentary layer that covers the entire earth. Yes there are multitudes of fossils in the sedimentary layer.

HOW ABOUT ARTIFACTS OF THE PEOPLE THAT WERE DESTROYED IN THE FLOOD?

Answer: We would expect to find artifacts of the people that were destroyed in Noah's Flood.

Remember that the Genesis account of the Flood describes that man and animals died in the Flood. But there is no Biblical account whatsoever of structures beings destroyed in the Flood:

▶ All in whose nostrils was the breath of life, of all that was in the dry land, died."
Genesis 22:7

Genesis reports that the Flood waters were not quite as deep as one would have imagined. The waters covered the earth "Fifteen cubits upward" (Genesis 7:20), which is about 25 ½ feet.

So any structures made out of megalith stone likely would have survived. They may have been sloshed around so they may be somewhat damaged, pushed off to the side or rolled over onto their sides or could still be standing erect. There would remain small artifacts that were washed along by way of underwater currents that may be found piled up together. Some larger structures may have just been covered with a layer of soot or sand, when the waters drained off the land.

Brien Foerster < subject, recognized authority>:
Top quality material, readily available on his Website, the Internet and in Bookstores.

Today a number of private self-explorers of the ancient civilization ruins in Egypt, Peru and locations all over the globe, not necessarily Noah's Flood proponents, have made a remarkable and extraordinary discovery. They have discovered that features of the oldest of the megaliths were machined by high tech equipment not chiseled with a hammer.

These self-explorers, such as Brien Foerster, post their works and products on the Internet. And are available for purchase.

The proof is in the viewing: Upon viewing the precise features on these megalith stones it is clearly obvious that such precision cuttings and shapings were the result of high tech machining equipment.

So then, what would one expect to find out about megalith stones today if there was a Noah's Flood?
Answer: If there was a Noah's Flood then the oldest stone structures would evidence the higher technology of the pre-flood world. Then because of the loss of technology in Noah's Flood the more recent in time stone structures would be the "stone and chisel."

As years passed after the Flood then of course evidence of the return of technology, most likely to some extent different technology from pre-flood technology should be found.

If there was no Noah's Flood then you simply would expect consistency. The newer the stone structures then the higher the technical advancement exhibited in the stone.

The ancient high technology was lost with the pre-flood people that were lost in the Flood. It is not known whether any pre-flood technology was onboard the Ark. Noah and his sons having lived in the pre-flood world would have known all about the pre-flood technology, and would have certainly been able to recognize or identify any pre-flood technology before and after the flood.

Serapeum of Saqqara in Egypt

For example the Serapeum of Saqqara in Egypt near the Great Pyramid of Giza. There located in an underground cave are twenty-four (24) One Hundred Ton (100 ton) granite rectangular boxes in separate rooms.

The boxes are empty, about 70 tons each with lids that are about 30 tons each. There is no explanation as to how the granitite boxes could be in the underground cave because the boxes are too big to fit into the cave stone passageways.

The boxes could not have been made above ground then lowered into the underground cave rooms because the size of the granite boxes and lids are way too big to fit into the narrow passageways and neither could a box fit from outside a room into a room of the cave because the entrance to any room is too narrow for a box or lid to fit through the entrance to any room in the underground cave.

This is one of the puzzles of the Serapeum of Saqqara in Egypt that the granite boxes and lids are too large to fit into the passageways and to small to fit through the entrance of the rooms where the granite boxes and lids are presently located. There are twenty-four (24) of these boxes and lids.

There is another puzzle: The high technical machining required to produce the inside corners of the boxes.

There is no explanation as to how the precision inside corners of the boxes could have been machined so accurate and so smooth in ancient times. There is no explanation because even today there appears to be no such technology to produce such precision inside corners to the granite boxes.

The only possible explanation is than these granite boxes and granite lids are artifacts of the pre-flood population – lost high technology. A product of man-made technology lost with the destruction of the pre-flood population.

Forget the hi-tech ancient alien theories or highly evolved humans that are hiding somewhere. The Flood answers all these questions.

As of the date of writing Tune-In Heaven I do not know of any system to classify or identify pre-flood artifacts. And, I do not know of anyone working on developing a pre-flood identification guide or classification chart.

It would seem initially that there would be two (2) identifiers:
1.) Recent low technology on top, or replacing high tech.
2.) The usage of the structure made to fit a different purpose other than for a purpose involving advanced technology.

Modern theories backed by the government deny Noah's Flood and the elite God haters would ridicule anyone presenting true evidence of a pre-flood civilization. But they are not invincible. They are wrong and they know it.

There was a Flood. There was a pre-flood world. There are artifacts here today that survived the flood. This is really very exciting! There is much important work that needs done here, identifying and categorizing pre-flood artifacts. I fully expect the truth to come out.

Ken Ham, President, CEO, and Founder of Answers in Genesis
< subject, recognized authority>:
Top quality material, readily available on Answers in Genesis Website, the Internet and in Bookstores.
The Creation Museum, located in Petersburg, Kentucky operated by Answers in Genesis.
Facility, 75,000-square-foot. Life-size Noah's Arc, Star Gazer's Planetarium and state-of-the-art exhibits.
Website: creationmuseum.org

How many people were lost in Noah's Flood, the Deluge?
Answer: Four (4) Billion people:
Four (4) Billion people, estimated lost their lives in the Flood. This number is based on a higher growth rate due to the known extremely long life spans.

Calculating this number using modern times growth rate yields about 750 million people at the time of the Flood, which is still a lot of people! Even many, many, more people that most folks would have ever thought.

This answer was found in Answers in Genesis. Answers in Genesis is an apologetics ministry, dedicated to helping Christians defend their faith and proclaim the gospel of Jesus Christ. Answers in Genesis provides top of the line resources for solid Biblical and scientific answers.
Answers in Genesis, What Was the Pre-Flood Population Like? January 6, 2016

The Water Canopy:

We can further review Genesis to understand what the earth was like before and during the flood:

The creationist, flood believer, geologist taught that there was a water canopy around the earth from their study of Genesis, before the fabricated (made-up) geological column theory:

▶ And God made the firmament, and divided the waters, which were under the firmament from the waters, which were above the firmament: and it was so.
Genesis 1:7

There are a lot of different definitions for firmament, choose "sky or stars"

Under the firmament then there would have been small ponds and streams. Above then in the sky would have been a thin cloud layer, a water canopy that completely, smoothly surrounded the earth.

So before the Flood the earth was more level and the water canopy would have been like a consistent cloud covering all over the earth so the distribution of the rainwater would have been more regular.

No oceans. One continuous land mass. When Noah's Flood occurred this canopy collapsed (the windows of heaven were opened) and the water came down, this is the "Flood." Also called the "Deluge." At the same time the canopy collapsed, under the floodwaters, volcanoes erupted, "The fountains of the great deep broken up." (Genesis 7:11) On account of the volcanic activity under the floodwaters Tsunami waves would have been traveling around the globe.

CHAPTER 5
Truth

What was the effect of the Flood on life and any structures that would have existed?

Answer: Life destroyed, "All in whose nostrils was the breath of life, of all that was in the dry land, died." (Genesis 22:7).

Genesis reports no destruction to the structures of the ancient people who were destroyed.

How deep was the water of Noah's Flood?

Approximately 25½ feet deep. Calculated as follows: "Fifteen cubits" (Genesis 7:20) is approximately 25½ feet deep. A cubit is the length of the arm, from the elbow to the outstretched fingertips, which would have been about 20.5 inches or 55 cm. Which is also about 8 ½ yards or nearly 8 meters.

The waters were not everywhere quite as deep as one would have imagined, approximately only 25½ feet deep. Consider that the entire globe was under water at various depths.
No depth less than 25½ feet deep.

That was a large volume of water. Land being pushed down caused mountains to be pushed up. Then the water drained off of the land forming great canyons and now the water is our oceans.

So any structures made out of megalith stone could have survived. Of course they were thrust and jostled around. Many utterly destroyed but others would have survived having been damaged, twisted around or on their side or standing upright. Some such structures could even be standing on the now dry land! Others would be buried under the land near the surface, covered in silt or sand. And still other structures in the oceans or near the earth's poles.

Huge megalithic artifacts could be found anywhere around the world. Small artifacts as well may have accumulated in common areas from receding flood currents likewise would be found anywhere in the world.

CHAPTER 5
Truth

Genesis 7, Biblical account of Noah's Flood:

▶ 16. And they that went in, went in male and female of all flesh, as God had commanded him: and the Lord shut him in.

17. And the flood was forty days upon the earth; and the waters increased, and bare up the ark, and it was lift up above the earth.

18. And the waters prevailed, and were increased greatly upon the earth; and the ark went upon the face of the waters.

19. And the waters prevailed exceedingly upon the earth; and all the high hills, that were under the whole heaven, were covered.

20. Fifteen cubits upward did the waters prevail; and the mountains were covered.

21. And all flesh died that moved upon the earth, both of fowl, and of cattle, and of beast, and of every creeping thing that creepeth upon the earth, and every man:

22. All in whose nostrils was the breath of life, of all that was in the dry land, died.

23. And every living substance was destroyed which was upon the face of the ground, both man, and cattle, and the creeping things, and the fowl of the heaven; and they were destroyed from the earth: and Noah only remained alive, and they that were with him in the ark.

24. And the waters prevailed upon the earth an hundred and fifty days.

Genesis 7: 16-24

Genesis 8, Biblical account of Noah's Flood:

1. And God remembered Noah, and every living thing, and all the cattle that was with him in the ark: and God made a wind to pass over the earth, and the waters assuaged;

2. The fountains also of the deep and the windows of heaven were stopped, and the rain from heaven was restrained;

3. And the waters returned from off the earth continually: and after the end of the hundred and fifty days the waters were abated.

4. And the ark rested in the seventh month, on the seventeenth day of the month, upon the mountains of Ararat.

5. And the waters decreased continually until the tenth month: in the tenth month, on the first day of the month, were the tops of the mountains seen.

6. And it came to pass at the end of forty days, that Noah opened the window of the ark, which he had made:

7. And he sent forth a raven, which went forth to and fro, until the waters were dried up from off the earth.

8. Also he sent forth a dove from him, to see if the waters were abated from off the face of the ground;

9. But the dove found no rest for the sole of her foot, and she returned unto him into the ark, for the waters were on the face of the whole earth: then he put forth his hand, and took her, and pulled her in unto him into the ark.

10. And he stayed yet other seven days;
and again he sent forth the dove out of the ark;

11. And the dove came in to him in the evening; and, lo, in her mouth was an olive leaf pluckt off: so Noah knew that the waters were abated from off the earth.

12. And he stayed yet other seven days; and sent forth the dove; which returned not again unto him any more.

Genesis 8, Biblical account of Noah's Flood (continued):

13. And it came to pass in the six hundredth and first year, in the first month, the first day of the month, the waters were dried up from off the earth: and Noah removed the covering of the ark, and looked, and, behold, the face of the ground was dry.

14. And in the second month, on the seven and twentieth day of was the earth dried the month,

15. And God spake unto Noah, saying,

16. Go forth of the ark, thou, and thy wife, and thy sons, and thy sons' wives with thee.

Genesis 8

The waters were not everywhere quite as deep as one would have imagined, approximately only 25½ foot deep. Consider that the entire globe was under water.

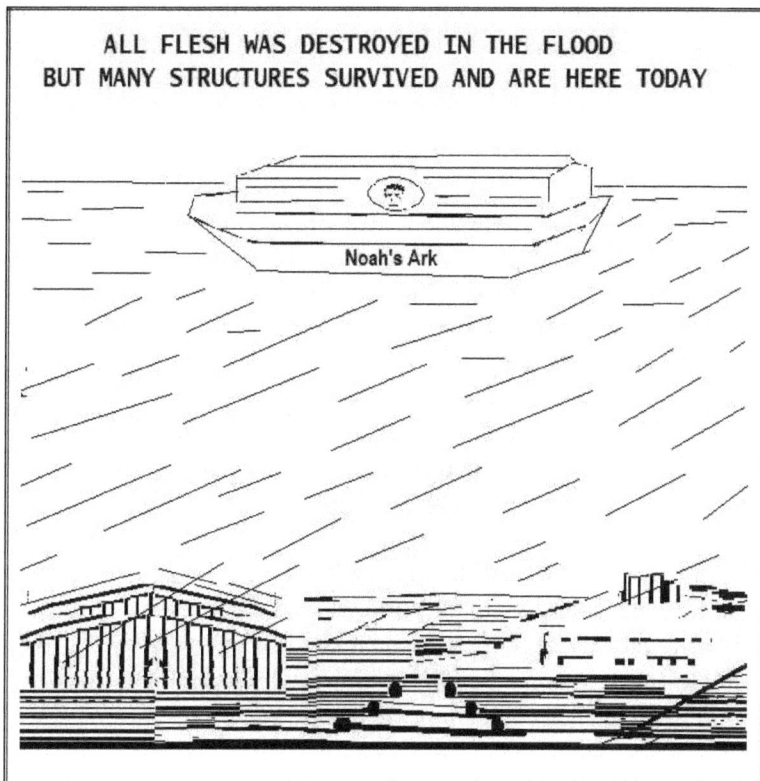

ALL FLESH WAS DESTROYED IN THE FLOOD
BUT MANY STRUCTURES SURVIVED AND ARE HERE TODAY

Noah's Ark

Truth Matters:

The Evidence supports Noah's Flood.

You cannot benefit from false doctrine. Believing in the lie that the earth is as it always was, shaped from the same geological events occurring in the past that occur today is going to hamper your faith.

If Noah's Flood did not happen then that is hard on the Bible.

Remember the champions of the Bible and Jesus Himself believed in Noah's Flood. Four (4) billion people, approximately died in the Flood. Many of their structures are being discovered today. Many megaliths and artifacts exhibit lost high technology. No ancient aliens, no inter-dimensional beings and no lost race of high intellects.
Noah's Flood explains it all!

The amount of years that elapsed from the Creation to the Flood can be determined from the Bible to be approximately 1,656 years. Four (4) billion people over 1,656 years would have developed high technology which could be quite different that ours.

Truth matters regarding outside influences that shapes our beliefs, desires and decisions to make specific choices.
Lies, false doctrines lead us astray!

Believing in the Truth helps us to choose the good things in our heart and give thanks and obey His commandments to tune in heaven and for us to enter into the Joy of the Lord, the Holy One who is the Higher Spirit who is the Creator of the Universe and receive His blessings.

HISTORY:
CLASSICAL HISTORY OR
MODERN DAY NATURAL HISTORY

This is presented first so that you know that there is a classic history of the world because you only hear the other side. You do not need to get this material down pat it is presented to acquaint you with principal truths and to expose modern false doctrines.

You cast away the deceptions and capture the truth and hold truth in the heart where truth shapes desires and shapes decisions that lead us into the Joy of the Lord, the Creator of the Universe, the Higher Spirit, the Holy One and Tune into Heaven and receive His Blessings.

God created the universe and man in six literal days and rested on the seventh day. There, truly was an actual Adam and Eve and a Garden of Eden that existed before the Flood. Remember that it was about 1,656 years from Creation to the Flood. Adam and Eve our great grandparents were cast out of the Garden. Banned from the Garden they lived in the pre-flood world. Then they had children, and their children had children and because of their extremely long life spans the population has been estimated up to Four (4) Billions people!

Right before the Flood in Genesis 9, Noah and his Wife had three sons: Shem, Ham, and Japheth, then before the Flood the Lord set man's days at 120 years. The Flood destroyed all the people except for Noah and his family. Noah's sons had sons. Noah, his sons, and their sons are referred to as the Table of Nations. The family migrated to Iraq from where the Arc rested on a mountain in Turkey, about a 400 mile distance. This area is known today pretty much in the center of what is called Mesopotamia.

Mesopotamia was the land between the two rivers, the Tigris and Euphrates. In or near Mesopotamia was the Plain of Shiner. The populations grew and spread over the entire globe, Africa, India, the Americas, the four corners of the world.

History records the first ancient civilizations of Sumer and Chaldea in Mesopotamia also known as the Cradle of Civilization and the Fertile Crescent. The people of Sumer the Sumerians were the Amorites, the sons of Canaan, the son of Ham, recorded in the Bible (Genesis 14:7).

The civilizations of Egypt, Ancient Israel, Phoenicia and Syria were next. Then the four great empires in sequence are Babylon, Persia, Greece then the Roman Empire. The British, Spanish, French and Germans colonized the Americas. World War 1 and World Ward 2 were fought. This is an outline of classic History.

Many if not all the world cultures have accounts of Adam and Eve and the Flood. The names of Adam and Eve are different in different cultures and the Flood stories vary.

Tower of Babel

Before the Flood and for a short time after the Flood for a few generations there was only one language. After the Flood at the Tower of Babel (today near Baghdad, Iraq) the Lord confused the language and the people could not understand one another's speech. That was the beginning of different languages. Different languages have different words for the same thing so therefore different names for Adam and Eve.

The apparent reason for the accounts of Adam and Eve and the Flood varying is that for everywhere, the descendants of Noah and his sons, other than the Bible, verbally passed down these major events to the younger family members. The accounts were passed down by the "around the campfire" type, the "story type" of re-telling of these great events.

Whereas, the Bible is the true account, divinely inspired word of the Lord. We have the correct account of Adam and Eve and the Flood through Moses, who authored Genesis, inspired by the Lord, the Holy One who is the Higher Spirit who is the Creator of the Universe.

Moses led his people out of the Egyptian captivity through the miracles of God almighty, the Red Sea parted and the Israelites walked through to the other side. Then the Red Sea closed on the pursuing Egyptian military and they were drowned. The Israelites were fed Manna from Heaven for forty years in the wilderness.

The Lord, the Holy One who is the Higher Spirit who is the Creator of the Universe gave Moses the Ten Commandments. The Bible is the correct account.

MODERN DAY NATURAL HISTORY

The modern day natural history approach is presented as a contrast and to expose the deceptions. You need to know they have no evidence for these theories. Again you do not need to get this material down pat. It is presented so you know there is a massive amount of evidence against the modern day natural history.

DOGMA:

The fist deception is dogma. We are taught dogma in public schools. Government schools are a better term for them.

Dogma simply means that their theories are required to be accepted. No choice in the matter. You must accept what is being taught. Otherwise, you are told you are wrong and you will be humiliated!

I can relate a hypothetical story of a hypothetical fourth grade girl in class telling the teacher that her father told her that milk is not good because it causes phlegm in the lungs. The teacher then led the class in repeating over and over again "Dana's dad is dumb" and made her cry. Oh yeah we all know these stories of how inquisitive minds are quieted.

But guess what: God gave us inquisitive minds.

It is ok to think. It is ok to disagree with one another especially these authoritarians. But not ok to show it in government school. Keep your mouth shut! Keep your mouth shut and pass the class. The Lord will put others in your life with whom you can debate and learn and develop to be intellectually persuasive not an authoritarian with a club!

MANIPULATION/WITCHCRAFT

You can only change yourself. Trying to change others is not
Biblical. The Lord gave us the ability to make decisions.
Trying to control or force yourself on others is manipulation.
Trying to change someone through the spiritual world is
witchcraft.

We are called upon to share the Word and take the Gospel to
the ends of the earth. We must be an example, loving and
convincing and ready when called upon to give an answer as
Apostle Peter said:

▶ But sanctify the Lord God in your hearts: and be ready
always to give an answer to every man that asketh you a
reason of the hope that is in you with meekness and fear.

1 Peter 3:15

You must know the Truth to advocate God's word. But is
also very helpful to know where the falseness is hidden in
these modern natural theories to be able to expose and
counter them with the truth. Remember share with those who
ask for knowledge. Otherwise do not push these beliefs on
others. You must always be a good example.

The Big Bang theory

The Big Bang theory is presented here to expose the deceptions and acquaint you with the voluminous material available today against modern day natural history. Hold in your heart the truth and cast out these lies.

Here is the Big Bang theory: In the beginning there was absolutely nothing, not even time. Then for a reason that not anyone even knows why a very slight quiver started vibrating. This quiver gave way to a strong vibration that became more and more intense. Then again for a reason that not anyone knows, the vibration started to explode. Out of the exploding vibrations of nothingness came into existence worlds, suns, solar systems and galaxies. And, the universe is still expanding today. Then in the future someday the universe will collapse into an infinitive point, and the cycle repeats.

Edwin Hubble popularized the Big Bang theory by postulating his "red shift" theory. Just like with the Doppler effect in sound.

The Doppler effect or Doppler shift is experienced by someone hearing the sound located somewhere other than on the moving source that is creating the sound, like a train. The one located somewhere other than on the train hears the sound of the train pitch change. When the train is moving away the sound waves gets stretched out causing the drop in tone sound effect: The longer the wavelength the lower the pitch. When the train is moving towards the listener, then the sound waves gets compressed causing the rise in tone sound effect: The shorter the wavelength the higher the pitch.

CHAPTER 5
Truth

Red Shift:

So comparatively as to the Doppler effect, the red shift theory postulates that as objects are moving away then the light shifts to the right. If an object would be moving towards us then the object would have a blue shift. With telescopes this red shift can be observed in every star, every galaxy and every celestial body. Therefore according to the red shift theory everything is moving away from the earth and nothing is moving towards the earth so therefore the universe is expanding. But is this red shift theory true and does this red shift theory prove the universe is expanding?

There are a lot of problems with the big bang theory and the red shift. First problem with the big bang expanding universe is "relativity." If everything is exploding/expanding at the same rate then the expansion could not be noticed. As I keep getting bigger the earth keeps getting bigger at the same rate. So does the sun, the moon, the space between us and so on and so on. Since we are all getting bigger at the same rate then we would appear the same size to one another. No expansion then would be noticed.

The explanation to save the big bang theory to this challenge is that the big bang expansion is not uniform it is like pennies on a balloon being pumped up - the pennies would not stretch with the balloon.

The Earth is in the Center of the Universe

All the telescopes everywhere observe all the stars, galaxies and celestial bodies exhibiting a red shift. So the telescopes indicate red shift, everything is moving away and no blue shift then nothing moving towards us. So then the earth is in the center of the universe.

You may need to reflect on this for a minute. If all we see is red shift and red shift means it is moving away then everything is moving away from us. No blue shift then nothing is moving towards the earth. So then we are in the center of the universe under this red shift theory.

There is no way the big bang promoters will accept the earth is in the center of the universe. This gets them hot under the collar. One may wonder why the big bang promoters hate the idea that the earth is in the center of the universe.

Why do the Big Bang Theory Advocates Hate the Earth in the Center of the Universe?

Answer: We can speculate as to why that gets them so mad is that it sounds like the earth may be important to the Lord if it is in the center of the universe. Modern day naturalist atheists will not accept any theory that allows room for God. Again remember it is not good to tease or torment big bang believers with this knowledge. Teach in love.

Can anything more Complex Result from an Explosion?

Answer: No:

Another problem with the big bang theory is clearly understood by an example: Let us say you blow up with mega dynamite a motor vehicle scrap yard that is full of metal scrap, a big explosion, would such an explosion ever result in producing a computer? Answer: No.
How about a satellite? Answer: No.

No matter how many times you explode the metal scrap yard, or how much dynamite or high explosive is detonated you will not produce a computer or a satellite, right? Nothing ever of more complexity ever comes out of an explosion.
Instead an explosion creates heat like a fire, everything gets blown to bits! Never is anything created more complex than what is blown up. What is blown up gets reduced to smaller bits!

So then how did an entire universe that is vastly complex come out of an explosion?
Answer: No way!

More Unanswerable Questions for Deniers of the Lord.
Questions not answerable by the Big Bang Theory:

If the big bang created time then how could time have been created before time was created?

How about an explanation as to how the big bang explosion created time?

How about a real explanation as to how anything could come out nothing before explaining how absolutely everything (the universe) came out of absolutely nothing?

Evolution:

I am going to cut to the chase here because I think you are getting the idea that these theories, which are referred to as "Natural Theories" have only one goal and that is to deny the Lord, the Holy One who is the Higher Spirit who is the Creator of the Universe.

So it becomes clear that the consequence of accepting such theories that deny the Lord would shape our decisions and influence our beliefs and our desires and what we hold in our hearts and then these beliefs held in our heart will attract the curses not the Blessings.

First problem with evolution:

When did non-life become life?

Answer: Their phony answer is billions of years and then life.

Under the big bang theory only matter was created. The big bang theory does not suggest life being created out of the big bang. Life came later on. So at some point in time under the big bang theory, under the naturalist theory plain matter had to become life.

This is unacceptably explained under the natural theories that so much time had to pass, that it took time, lots of time, billions of years and then life occurred. Which does not answer the question as to how did matter become life? There is no explanation as to how a strand of life could come to life out of physical, plain, lifeless matter. No, not volcanoes or gasses or explosions or lightning strikes, no hope for monsters, no fairy tales, no science fiction.

Major problem with evolution:

Is it possible for evolution to have occurred?

Answer: No. There is no evidence that the process of evolution has occurred even once. And, the theory requires it to repeat countless times over millions of years. The theory is total nonsense!

First, slow down the theory of evolution and walk through it:

Let us take a hypothetical animal from the past such as a cow-like creature evolving into a whale. Their theory, not mine. It starts out with one of these cow-like creatures, a bull develops shorter legs as a genetic defect lets say living on the North Beach.

In order for that trait to pass-on to the next generation the bull has to meet a heifer, a female cow with the same genetic defect lets say from on the South Beach and then they would have offspring with shorter legs.

Then these offspring would need to mate within the group of offspring with shorter legs or with other cows that developed this shorter leg genetic defect lets say from on the West Beach. Then a herd of shorter legs cow-like creatures develops.

Next out of this herd of shorter legs cow-like creatures one of them experiences a genetic defect and has even shorter legs. For this even shorter legs trait to pass-on to the next generation that animal has to meet a mate with this even shorter yet legs, same genetic defect.

So then this animal would have to breed with another animal that had the same defect. Then a herd of even shorter legs cow-like creatures develops.

And so on and so on then until you have an animal with no legs trying to breed with another animal with no legs? Would not predators devour such cow-like creatures with no legs lying on the beach?

So then let us suppose that this animal with no legs mated with another animal with no legs. Suppose that this really happened. Next a herd would have to come about. Really? Then it would take numerous genetic defects and generations of mating to produce a whale. How is that possible? Finally then the whale could swim away into the Ocean.

But wait! What about a mate for the whale? Where does the mate for the whale come from? They would have to say that the same process described above had to occur somewhere else during the same timeline to produce a genetically perfect mate for the whale!

Transitional Animal Fossils

Are there any such transisionary forms in the Fossil Record?

Answer: No fossils of any transisionary forms for any animal.

Under such an evolutionary theory requiring millions of years one would expect to find numerous skeleton fossils of "transisionary forms," in the fossil record. That is skeleton fossils of animals exhibiting the transitional stage of the particular stage in the sequence of changing from one stage to another stage in the evolutionary development of the evolving animal into becoming another animal: Like all the cow-like animals with ever increasingly shorter legs in transition into becoming a whale. Over millions of years, as they say, there should be thousands maybe millions of such skeletal fossils. There is zero.

Evolution Theory: before chromosomes were known.

The popularization of evolution was through the publication of "On the Origin of Species," authored by Charles Darwin, published in 1859, before DNA, before chromosomes, before Gregor Mendel published his work on pea plants in 1866.

Back then they believed acquired traits passed on to their offspring. Example: A husband and wife develop endurance and speed in running then this would pass on to their offspring who would be born with this ability to be fast runners!

Charles Darwin was known for reflecting on the theory of evolution of the eye because of the recent development of the camera in his day. He wondered how an eye could have happened by chance when it did not appear possible to him that such a complicated instrument as a camera (and in his day it was pretty basic) could happen by chance. Could a lightning bolt strike the beach turning the glass into a lens and turning the driftwood into a case creating a camera? No.

Also back then they believed in spontaneous generation such as stirring mud would generate worms or that eventually in a pond, fish would be generated (spontaneous generation,) which we know today, is not possible. Also the whale that swam away had to be fully formed. Even if the flapper on the air blow tube were not fully formed the whale would have drowned the first time it dived down in the water because it would have taken on water.

CHAPTER 6

~

Why Believe in Christianity?

Blessings, Prosperity, the Protection, the Joy of God Almighty, the Higher Power the Creator God, the Good Heavenly Father, the Holy One, the Redeemer.

Salvation. God loves you and wants to have a personal relationship with you forever, eternal life.

Joy. He will take away misery and give you joy that passes all understanding.

Blessings. The believer will receive blessings, the Lord's favor, prosperity, achievement and joy here on earth and as well in heaven for eternity.

Wisdom. The fear of the Lord is the beginning of knowledge. If the believer asks for knowledge he will receive knowledge.

Personal fulfillment. One can find his or her purpose in life.

Choose Christianity. Choose Christianity/Choose life for you and your descendents. Choose another way you choose death. Set before you are life and death, blessing and curses: therefore choose life. There never was since the fall of man, more than one way to heaven. Call upon the Name of the Lord and repent.

<u>Jesus Christ is our Savior</u>. Call upon the name of the Lord, the Lord of Abraham, Isaac and Jacob, with your mouth, repent, confess your sins, thank the Lord Jesus, for dying for your sins and believe in your heart that God has raised Jesus from the dead, you will be saved. You are saved by the sacrifice of Jesus on the cross. You cannot earn salvation through your own works. Jesus loves you while you are yet a sinner and He awaits your repentance.

<u>You can trust the Bible Translations</u>: <u>Reliability</u>. The Bible is the account, the historic record of God's reaching out to His people.

CHAPTER 7

~
You Can Trust the Bible

You can trust the Bible Translations: Reliability.

The Bible is the true account, the historic record of God reaching out to His people.

Written by individuals who were inspired and were personal witnesses to God. Their writings written over 1,600 years were assembled into our sixty-six books, Bible.

We can look back today from our present viewpoint and see who wrote these books of the Bible and how the Bible was written. To really understand the Bible we have to look from the experience of the writers as they were witnessing and experiencing of our Lord. Each person, who wrote a part of the Bible, wrote from a specific time and place in history. CAUTION: Be careful of your sources. Thoroughly evaluate the source, compare with other sources and compare to the Bible (King James Version or the Geneva Bible).

The New Testament:

Two of the disciples of Jesus wrote two of the Gospels. The Gospel of Matthew and the Gospel of John were written by Matthew and John two of the twelve disciples of Jesus.

The other two Gospels, the Gospel of Mark and the Gospel of Luke were written by first-hand associates of the disciples of Jesus.

The Gospel of Mark was written by Mark a disciple of Peter. Peter was one of the twelve disciples of Jesus. Mark founded the Coptic Orthodox Church of Alexandria, the largest Christian Church in Egypt and Northeast Africa.

The Gospel of Luke was written by Luke who was well educated, a physician and a respected historian who traveled with the Apostle Paul. Luke interviewed and observed the Apostle Paul and other apostles including Apostle Peter, Apostle John and others of the early church. Luke also wrote the Acts of the Apostles known as Acts.

The New Testament also includes letters, which were written by the Apostle Paul, the Apostle Peter, and the Apostle John. Christians have good reason to be confident of the reliability and authenticity of the New Testament. These are first hand accounts!

The Old Testament:
There are more than 14,000 existing Old Testament manuscripts and also the Dead Sea Scrolls that agree precisely with the present day Bible. The language of the Old Testament was Aramaic and Hebrew (similar languages). Abraham, for example, most likely spoke Aramaic.

Moses wrote the first five (5) Books of the Bible. There were many other writers, such as David, Joshua, Jeremiah and other prophets.

The Bible is true, recorded history. The Bible is also God's law, wisdom, poetry and prophesy. There is widespread evidence for the absolute reliability of the Bible. The Bible was written over a period of time spanning at least 1,600 years, written from 1445 B.C to 90 A.D.

The Septuagint:

Then, after Alexander the Great's military conquests the ancient world became Greek-speaking.

According to Jewish authorities six Jewish scholars from each of the twelve tribes of Israel independently translated the Old Testament Scriptures into Greek. When they were all finished to the amazement of all there were no discrepancies among the translations.

Because six (6) times twelve (12) is seventy-two (72), roughly seventy, later the Latin term for seventy, Septuagint, became the name of this translation of the Old Testament.

The Septuagint translation from Hebrew to Greek occurred some time during the third century B.C. Hebrew scribes dedicated their lives to preserving the accuracy of these Holy Jewish Scriptures. In addition, the ancient scrolls and manuscripts discovered and in existence today totally agree with the Septuagint.

The Vulgata Bible:

Then during the Roman Empire, around 400 A.D., Jerome translated the Bible into Latin. The Latin translation became known as the "Vulgate" from Latin name versio vulgata, meaning in Latin: "commonly used translation."

Gutenberg Bible:

With the beginning of the printing press the quantity of Bibles in circulation vastly increased. Most notably the "Gutenberg Bible" which was the Jerome translated Latin Vulgate edition of Bible that was printed in Latin at Mainz, Germany by Johannes Gutenberg from 1452 –1455.

Wycliffe Bible:

John Wycliffe translated the Vulgate from Latin into an English version prior to the printing press in 1380 through 1388. This English version was produced before the invention of the printing press and hence all original copies are hand written. The first printed edition was not produced until 1731.

Geneva Bible:

The Geneva Bible was printed in 1560 in English. Although the Geneva Bible is not well known today it was the Bible brought to America in the Mayflower, it is the Bible upon which America was founded. The Geneva Bible was the "Bible of the Protestant Reformation" and the Bible of the Puritans and Pilgrims, the Bible of most early American colonists, who were fleeing religious oppression.

The Geneva Bible was state-of-the-art in its day - it was the first English Bible to use verse numbers and extensive commentary. The Geneva Bible contained study aids, illustrations, maps and indexes of names and topics, and marginal notes. Each chapter has a list of contents with verse numbers.

The New Testament of the Geneva Bible was translated from scholarly works, which were substantially based on translations by William Tyndale and Myles Coverdale.

The Geneva Bible was the first English version in which all of the Old Testament was translated directly from the Hebrew. In the late sixteenth century the Geneva Bible was affordable to even the lowest-paid laborers.

It is interesting to note the historical backdrop of the Geneva Bible. Queen Mary I was the daughter of King Henry VIII. The Pope of the Roman Catholic Church had refused King Henry VIII a divorce from Mary's mother.

In order to accomplish his divorce and remarriage King Henry VIII had all of England break away from the Roman Catholic Church. Following a time of turmoil in England, then Queen Mary I obtained the crown and she desired to return England to the Roman Catholic Church. Mary I, also known as "Bloody Mary," banned English Bibles and persecuted Protestants. Many fled from England and many of those Protestants settled in Geneva, Switzerland, including John Calvin, hence the name Geneva Bible.

King James Version, Bible, Year: 1611

The King James Version was written by inspired men who sought the truth rather than their own praise. After seven years approximately, six teams of fifty-four men, men who were chosen were the best biblical scholars and linguists of their day. Also the King James Version had the unwavering support of King James of England and Bishop Bancroft.

The translation was from the original Greek and Hebrew manuscripts as opposed to a translation into English from the Latin Vulgate.

From the middle of the seventeenth century through present times, the King James's Bible has been the most recognized version of the Bible, which was translated into English and was printed in 1611.

Most notably: The King James Version is a precision match with the Geneva Bible without any sort of attempt to match them up.

The Martin Luther Bible

Also in the mid 1500's Martin Luther and others translated the Bible into the common German language of the day. The Luther Bible is a German language Bible translated from Hebrew and ancient Greek by Martin Luther, of which the New Testament was printed in 1522 and the completed Bible, containing both the Old and New Testaments and Apocrypha was printed in 1534.

Present Day Bible Translations:

Present day translations are either Word for Word or Thought for Thought type translations. Much insight can be gained from reading the same Bible book, chapter and verse in the different translations.

I personally recommend the primary source of Bible reading the King James Version or the Geneva Bible.

Bible Divine Creditability:

No other holy book even comes close to the Bible in the amount of evidence supporting its credibility, authenticity and divine authorship. There are over 2,000 prophecies in the Old Testament that have already been fulfilled, of which there are over 300 fulfilled prophecies that deal with the Messiah fulfilled in Jesus Christ.

The message of the cross is foolishness to those who are perishing, but to the saved, it is the power of God.

▶ For the preaching of the cross is to them that perish foolishness; but unto us which are saved it is the power of God.
1 Corinthians 1:18

Bible Versions and Bible History

Professor Walter J Veith, Seventh-Day-Adventist, Author, Biblical, Educational Material Producer, Researcher, Nutritionist, Authoritative Lectures:
< subject, recognized authority>

Professor Veith produces in-depth, well-researched and documented material regarding the Bible, and for information regarding Bible Versions/Bible history consider highly educational any material produced by Professor Walter Veith. Top quality material, readily available on Amazing Discoveries, Seventh Day Adventist, Website, his Website, the Internet and in Bookstores.

Critics are easily rebuked: Contrary to what you hear over the mass media television news complex there is ample defenses to any challenges to the Bible and to the Faith of Christianity.

Do not settle for an answer that denies the creditability of the Bible or the Faith: Research, research and research on. Now with the Internet, continue to research and you can find the answers. There is an answer to every challenge to the Bible and to Faith. There are answers that are clear and convincing, that overwhelm the skeptics. There are logical arguments, which support the Bible and the Faith, and now modern technology provides empirical evidences to prove-up the Bible and the Faith.

NOTE: If what is being said contradicts the Bible and you do have a defense that does not mean what is being said is true.

Also, a caveat – Never accept what is said to be "in the Bible" without locating the passage in the Bible and verifying it as "in the Bible." Reference the King James Version or Geneva Bible. Then read the entire chapter to understand the passage in context. Bible search software and the Internet are great tools. It is a great time to be a Christian.

Paul and Silas preached in Berea and Thessalonica, two cities in northern Greece. Christians from Berea were praised for their known devotion to "search the scriptures."

▶ 10. And the brethren immediately sent away Paul and Silas by night unto Berea: who coming thither went into the synagogue of the Jews.

11. These were more noble than those in Thessalonica, in that they received the word with all readiness of mind, and searched the scriptures daily, whether those things were so.

12. Therefore many of them believed; also of honourable women, which were Greeks, and of men, not a few.

Acts 17: 10-12

CHAPTER 8

~

Understanding God

If there is any quality that would make God the one true God it is that God has to be the "Creator God."

Anything that exists in our world cannot self-create itself from within this world. Something in a picture cannot not create itself from within the picture. A room in your house cannot create itself from the house. God is outside of his creation, this universe. He is outside of time, space and energy. He is outside of his creation like the artist is outside the picture. The difference between a human artist and God is that God can supernaturally come into his creation.

God walked with man in the Garden of Eden until the fall of mankind (Adam and Eve ate the forbidden fruit). He reached out to mankind through prophets, Noah, Abraham, Jacob, and then he came into his creation through Jesus Christ.

He became both God and man. Jesus is Truth, the Word (the Word of God is the Bible), redemption, sins forgiven and eternal life. Jesus is the Higher Spirit, the Good Heavenly Father, the Holy One, the Creator, the Protector, God Almighty the Redeemer the Good Shepherd, and Jesus knows His own and His own know Him

▶ 14. I am the good shepherd, and know my sheep, and am known of mine.

15. As the Father knoweth me, even so know I the Father: and I lay down my life for the sheep.

John 10: 14-15.

You know in your heart Jesus is Lord. As you read through the Gospels, Mathew, Mark, Luke or John, in the New Testament you recognize that the red lettered text, the quoted words as the words of our savior, Jesus.

Salvation a Gift from God

We cannot earn salvation. It is a gift from the Lord. When we repent of our sin the Lord hears and forgives then we receive the Lord Jesus Christ as our personal Lord and Savior, our sins are forgiven. We receive His blessings. We thereafter have a personal fellowship with the Lord.

We turn to trust, praise and delight and commit our way to the Lord and that assures receiving the good desires of our heart, blessings, prosperity, and the protection of God Almighty, the Protector and entering into the Joy of the Lord, the Higher Power, the Creator God, the Holy One, the Redeemer:

▶ 3. Trust in the Lord, and do good; so shalt thou dwell in the land, and verily thou shalt be fed.

4. Delight thyself also in the Lord: and he shall give thee the desires of thine heart.

Psalm 37: 3-4

When we turn to trust, praise and delight and commit our way to the Lord then that is being in accordance with his Will. If we ask anything in accordance with His will, we have His Promise that we get what we asked of Him.

▶ 14. And this is the confidence that we have in him, that, if we ask anything according to his will, he heareth us:

15. And if we know that he hear us, whatsoever we ask, we know that we have the petitions that we desired of him.

1 John 5: 14-15

Do you want a life of purpose and hope?

The Lord loves us while we are in sin. Jesus died for our sins. God, the one who created you, has a purpose for your life and wants to give you a fresh start. As described in Apostle Paul's Letter to the Romans:

▶ 6. For when we were yet without strength, in due time Christ died for the ungodly.

7. For scarcely for a righteous man will one die: yet peradventure for a good man some would even dare to die.

8. But God commendeth his love toward us, in that, while we were yet sinners, Christ died for us.

9. Much more then, being now justified by his blood, we shall be saved from wrath through him.

10. For if, when we were enemies, we were reconciled to God by the death of his Son, much more, being reconciled, we shall be saved by his life.

11. And not only so, but we also joy in God through our Lord Jesus Christ, by whom we have now received the atonement.

12. Wherefore, as by one man sin entered into the world, and death by sin; and so death passed upon all men, for that all have sinned:

13. For until the law sin was in the world: but sin is not imputed when there is no law.

14. Nevertheless death reigned from Adam to Moses, even over them that had not sinned after the similitude of Adam's transgression, who is the figure of him that was to come.

15. But not as the offence, so also is the free gift. For if through the offence of one many be dead, much more the grace of God, and the gift by grace, which is by one man, Jesus Christ, hath abounded unto many.

Romans 5:6-15

The Sinner's Prayer

Dear Jesus, I call upon Your name Jesus, God Almighty, the Good Heavenly Father, the Higher Power the Creator God, the God of the Universe, the Holy One, the Holy Spirit, the Redeemer, the God of Abraham, Isaac and Jacob.

Thank you for convicting me of sin, in my mind, in my heart and in my actions. You loved me while I was still in sin. I want to turn away from sin and commit my way to Your way, Lord and to trust in You, Lord. Please forgive me, I am genuinely sorry, I desire to do what is right from now on, help me avoid sinning again.

Good Heavenly Father, I need your help. Please save me from the bondage of sin, save me from the curses, frustration, confusion, loss, sorrow, heartaches, further consequences of sin/evil actions and end the repeating patterns and cycles.

I desire positive changes in my life, to receive the Blessings, and the Prosperity of the Good Heavenly Father, and the Protection of God Almighty, and the Joy of the Lord.

I believe that your son, Jesus Christ died for my sins, was resurrected from the dead, is alive, and hears my prayer. Please Jesus become the Lord of my life. Rule and reign in my heart from this day forward. Let Your Will be done through me. Holy Spirit come dwell in me to empower me to obey God's commandments.

In Jesus name I pray. Praise you Father, Son and Holy Spirit.

Thank you Jesus!

Amen.

If you chose to repent of sin and receive Christ today, congratulations! Now, as a way to grow closer to Him, the Bible tells us to follow up on our commitment. Read the Bible. Ask God to increase your faith and help your understanding of the Bible and to know Him better.

How to Read the Bible: Read the Bible like any other book. God is the "Great Communicator." The words mean what the common meaning of the words are defined and understood.

The Bible is a collection of sixty-six books, which comprise the Old and the New Testaments. The books of the Bible contains history accounts, wisdom, law, psalms (songs), hymns & poetry), epistles (letters) and prophesy.

The Old Testament books were written before Jesus Christ. The New Testament was written after the birth of Jesus. Jesus Christ is Lord. He is the source of grace and salvation. Proclaiming the redemption of Jesus is the Gospel. Gospel (originally Greek) means Good News. The Bible is the Word of the Lord.

You can pick-up the Bible and just start reading. Or here is my guideline:

First read Second Peter, which is a very short letter that outlines the Christian Faith and includes Peter affirming that he "was an eye witness to His majesty."

Reading the Gospels (Matthew, Mark, Luke, John) will make known to you Christ's life and ministry.

First gospel to read is Mark, it is clear, concise and the shortest Gospel.

Next read the gospel of Luke, which presents the account of Jesus' miraculous birth, ministry of healing and parables, passion, and resurrection. Then read the gospel of Mathew, which adds more of the teachings of Jesus. Or read next the Gospel of John and come back later to Luke and Matthew.

The Gospel of John: the Word became Flesh, the Spiritual Gospel, asking how do we know God: We know Jesus.
John personally walked with the living Jesus Christ. John recorded first-hand the events of Jesus.
John witnessed and testified to the Crucifixion, the Resurrection, and the Resurrected Jesus. The Gospel of John includes simple and clear passages and some of the deepest and most profound passages of the faith.

After that, you can read the Epistles (letters) of Paul to the early churches such as Galatians, Ephesians, and Philippians. Apostle Paul is explaining the Gospel to the early churches. The name of the epistle is the name of the city where the early church is located. What better way to learn the Word of the Lord than reading Apostle Paul explaining the Word to the early churches?

Remember, the key to understanding the Bible is asking God for wisdom and understanding. God is the author of the Bible, and He wants you to understand His Word.

CHAPTER 9

~

Leonard's Fireside Chat

Pull-up alongside and pour yourself a cup of coffee or other favorite beverage as you please and praise and give thanks to the Lord. You can find delight in following the Lord's commandments. The seven precepts are life-changing if you really take them to heart. The underlying, two essential precepts that you must learn is to stop complaining, and, whatever you hold in your heart is what the Lord will provide or allow for you.

If you hold Truth in your heart then you are holding Jesus in your heart. Jesus is the Truth. Jesus is the "Word:" The Word is the Bible. If you hold true doctrines in your heart like Creation, Noah's Flood and the Bible you are holding Jesus in your heart.

Whereas if you believe false doctrines like the Big Bang Theory, Evolution and Gradualism, then you are filling up your heart with lies, delusions and misconceptions. As a result you attract evil/Satan into your heart. Whether witting or unwittingly the result is you experience the consequences of believing false doctrine. There is no benefit from such false doctrine. Life appears fortuitous. And worse, you are attracting curses, frustration, sorrow, and you risk the loss of the protection and the loss of a personal relationship with the Lord.

In summary:

The two core precepts:

To stop complaining, finding delight in following the Lord's commandments, giving thanks in all things, and,

The Lord's jurisdiction is the heart, whatever you hold in your heart then that is what the Lord will provide for you, or allow for you.

The other precepts, truth, the Lord is truth, the power to choose, always choose the right thing and do the right thing, that you can only change your own behavior, vengeance is the Lord's - the Lord redirects evil back to sender, means it for good, and many are saved, and you can have a personal relationship with the Lord, these seven precepts are wholly worthy to Tune in Heaven.

Not only will you receive the Blessings of the Good Heavenly Father, the Lord's Prosperity, the Protection of God Almighty, the Joy of the Lord, the Salvation of the Redeemer, Jesus promises to you that after the end of times to be in Heaven with the Lord.

The End of Times

In a letter written by Apostle Peter, describing after the Lord comes for his people, after the end of times, then the earth, the universe the elements of the universe, that is everything, will be dissolved in a fervent heat:

▶ 10. But the day of the Lord will come as a thief in the night; in the which the heavens shall pass away with a great noise, and the elements shall melt with fervent heat, the earth also and the works that are therein shall be burned up.

11. Seeing then that all these things shall be dissolved, what manner of persons ought ye to be in all holy conversation and godliness,

12. Looking for and hasting unto the coming of the day of God, wherein the heavens being on fire shall be dissolved, and the elements shall melt with fervent heat?

13. Nevertheless we, according to his promise, look for new heavens and a new earth, wherein dwelleth righteousness.

14. Wherefore, beloved, seeing that ye look for such things, be diligent that ye may be found of him in peace, without spot, and blameless.

15. And account that the longsuffering of our Lord is salvation; even as our beloved brother Paul also according to the wisdom given unto him hath written unto you;

16. As also in all his epistles, speaking in them of these things; in which are some things hard to be understood, which they that are unlearned and unstable wrest, as they do also the other scriptures, unto their own destruction.

17. Ye therefore, beloved, seeing ye know these things before, beware lest ye also, being led away with the error of the wicked, fall from your own stedfastness.

18. But grow in grace, and in the knowledge of our Lord and Saviour Jesus Christ. To him be glory both now and for ever. Amen.

2 Peter 3: 10 –18

If everything including the universe is going to be destroyed in a fervent heat then what about us?
Apostle Paul explains: "we will be changed:"

▶ … in a flash, in the twinkling of an eye, at the last trumpet. For the trumpet will sound, the dead will be raised imperishable, and we will be changed.

1 Corinthians 15: 52

At the End of Times all the former things will pass away and the Lord will make all things new: A new Jerusalem, where there will be no more death, neither sorrow, nor crying, neither shall there be any more pain.
Note: Biblical Symbology for Sea translates as People Note: Tabernacle is an older word for dwelling place, tent or coat.

Note: Heaven also means "Sky" as well as the "Dwelling of the Lord"

▶ 1. And I saw a new heaven and a new earth: for the first heaven and the first earth were passed away; and there was no more sea.

2. And I John saw the holy city, new Jerusalem, coming down from God out of heaven, prepared as a bride adorned for her husband.

3. And I heard a great voice out of heaven saying, Behold, the tabernacle of God [is] with men, and he will dwell with them, and they shall be his people, and God himself shall be with them, [and be] their God.

4. And God shall wipe away all tears from their eyes; and there shall be no more death, neither sorrow, nor crying, neither shall there be any more pain: for the former things are passed away.

5. And he that sat upon the throne said, Behold, I make all things new. And he said unto me, Write: for these words are true and faithful.

6. And he said unto me, It is done. I am Alpha and Omega, the beginning and the end. I will give unto him that is athirst of the fountain of the water of life freely.

7. He that overcometh shall inherit all things; and I will be his God, and he shall be my son.

Revelation 21: 1-7

The Disciple John encourages us with bearing witness to the words of Jesus as to what the hereafter will be like for us believers:

▶ 2. In my Father's house are many mansions: if it were not so, I would have told you. I go to prepare a place for you.

3. And if I go and prepare a place for you, I will come again, and receive you unto myself; that where I am, there ye may be also.

John 14: 2-3

The Apostle Paul encourages us regarding the hereafter:

▶ But as it is written, Eye hath not seen, nor ear heard, neither have entered into the heart of man, the things which God hath prepared for them that love him.

1 Corinthians 2:9

The Universe is the Persistence of the Word of the Lord.

We connect with the Lord, engage in a personal relationship with the Lord, the Higher Power, receive His blessings and enter into His Joy, the Holy One, the Creator God, the God Almighty, the Redeemer.

Scientific Theories are useful to explain our reality as long as they do not contradict the Word of the Lord, the Bible. Theories that do not contradict the Bible help us understand the Lord's Creation.

Do not get bogged down with this topic. Keep reading Tune-In Heaven. If you are not a "science theory type" just go ahead and skip down to the next topic: WHAT'S IN A NAME?

In the following I harmonize modern scientific theories, String Theory, Quantum Field Theory and Morphic Fields to align with the Word of the Lord: The Universe is the Persistence of the Word of the Lord.

After the Lord spoke the universe into existence the universe continues on, this outcome, our existing universe, I dare say to call this continuation of the universe: the Persistence of the Word of the Lord.

The Universe is the Persistence of the Word of the Lord is being outlined here, not being fully developed:

The String Theory theorizes that the smallest of all matter is infinitely small vibrating strings. In Genesis the Lord spoke the creation into existence. The universe continues to exist. The infinitely small vibrating strings are the persistence of the Word, the aftermath or the effect of His Word.

There is an important difference from the infinitely small vibrating strings (Sting Theory) as the after effects of the Word of the Lord from another very different concept that the Lord is everything, which is Pantheism. Pantheism is not Biblical. Pantheism is a belief that the universe and the divine are the same thing, therefore the Lord is everything. The universe under Pantheism is animated by the Lord, as a horse running is animated by the horse.

The Biblical understanding is that the Lord is like an artist who paints a picture. The power of our Lord is to enter into this "picture He painted" that picture is the universe we live in. The Lord comes and goes in this universe as He pleases.

Sinclair Lewis, a champion of the Christian faith, popular in the 1950's explained that the infinite mind of the Lord gives the Lord an infinite quantity of infinities, so the Lord can spend an infinity individually with each one of us.

The Events, the Occurrences of the Universe are Recorded into the Quantum Fields of Space:

Next: understanding the "Nothingness" of space as "fields" allows for all the events, the occurrences of the universe to be recorded into the quantum fields of space just like data is recorded onto the magnetic field of hard drives of computers:

First, the String Theory concept includes Quantum Fields. Quantum Fields are similar to magnetic and electric fields. The theories of magnetic and electric fields can best be illustrated by the lines of force that shape the iron sprinklings on a piece of glass when a magnet is placed underneath. The iron sprinklings exhibit the lines of flux of the magnetic field.

Physics teaches that these invisible fields shape, form, organize and manifests particles like electrons and photons. And, further theorizes that the concept of fields explains the vast gap between planets, stars and galaxies.

The "Nothingness" of empty space is described as "the Quantum Foam" of the quantum field. The quantum foam is the fabric of the universe, fluctuating, ever changing, subatomic particles and energy of space-time.

It would seem then that events as they occur would likewise be occurring in the quantum foam. Leaving not just a "footprint" in the quantum foam but events would be recorded in the quantum foam, the fabric of the universe. The recordings in the quantum foam, the fabric of the universe is like data recorded onto a "hard drive" on a computer.

CHAPTER 9
Leonard's Fireside Chat

Everything is being recorded in the quantum field, the fabric of the universe! Perhaps if the Lord does not come soon then "Reader/Players" will be invented that will read these recorded events and play them as a video. Viewing the recorded history, past events of the universe would then be like watching a video. You would not be able to interact with what you are watching as it has already occurred: Similar to watching a movie.

Think of the consequences of a Reader/Player that can show as a picture, video images or movie of some select past event from the recorded data in the fabric of the universe. No privacy. Anything that has ever occurred anywhere is recorded. Everything anyone has ever done is recorded. Therefore evidence of crimes would be obtainable.

Also you can see how demons could involve themselves with these recordings to beguile victims. Causing these recordings of deceased family members to be viewable to victims!

Also here is an explanation for ghost-like images that seem to float in another dimension that appear on surveillance cameras or elsewhere. Somehow an event that has been recorded into the quantum foam is being "read and played" into our viewing.

Also consider that data recorded on a computer hard drive can be altered, manipulated or edited. Could radiation, magnetic waves, plasma or electric current change the recorded data? What would be the effect if quantum field recordings were altered? Perhaps all recordings of that same event that were recorded by cameras, pictures, movies or tape players would also be altered to be in alignment with the fabric of the universe. The present or the future cannot be changed. But recorded data certainly can be altered.

Biological Morph Fields:

Rupert Sheldrake as previously discussed in Chapter 5, Truth, has put forth the proposition that there are Morphic Fields where animals and humans connect into according to their kind and their closeness to form groups. These morph fields shape, form and organize similarly to electric and magnetic fields. Our brain is like an antenna that receives, picks-up or reads morph fields.

Information is stored in the morph fields for life forms to access, similarly as there are quantum fields for non-life forms to access. Everything is being recorded into Morph Fields! Non-Biological events as well as Biological data!

Plants, animals and humans connect into their respective group morph fields. It would seem that individual members would have some sort of right to use, access, key that would allow members only access to the morph fields and restrict others from entering the morph field. Otherwise predators such as bears and wild cats would have access to the morph fields of their prey. Perhaps for humans a "Name" could be a key to gain access.

Rupert Sheldrake postulates that the respective group morph field is a forming and organizing biological field that provides developmental genetic instructions to individual members.

There is no "blueprint" or "schematic" in DNA or in the Genome. DNA, the double helix only provides instructions for protein formation, that is it. The arms and the legs contain the same proteins but they are quite different. DNA cannot explain the differences.

Not only is there no blueprint or schematic of the body in DNA neither is there any developmental instructions in DNA or the Genome. This can easily be verified by reviewing college level biology material. Even though they may claim early on such blueprint, schematic or map of the body nothing of the sort is every presented. Only the amino acid/protein codes of the ladder steps of the double helix is ever explained in detail.

Scientific Theories are useful to explain our reality as long as they do not contradict the Bible. Theories that do not contradict the Bible help us understand the Lord's creation.

We connect with the Lord, engage in a personal relationship with the Lord, the Higher Power, receive His blessings and enter into His Joy, the Holy One, the Creator God, the God Almighty, the Redeemer.

At the end of times the universe is dissolved in a fervent heat that melts the elements of the universe. The heavens are destroyed. There is no escaping into a morph field. The morph fields will be dissolved as well. Other than through Jesus there is no way to the Lord's kingdom. All others will perish.

The Lord is our only hope. Our Lord and His Kingdom is the only Lord worthy of serving. He is a Just, Fair and Loving God. Thank you Lord. Praise you Heavenly Father. God Bless.

WHAT'S IN A NAME?

Apparently, there is a lot of meaning in names. Why else would the Lord give someone a new name unless it had powerful purpose and consequential meaning? In the Bible individuals were given new names to represent a further purpose and meaning after events or experiences some examples include the following:

- Abram renamed Abraham
- Sarai renamed Sarah
- Jacob renamed Israel
- Simon renamed Peter
- Saul renamed Paul

Abram was renamed Abraham because he was destined be the father of a multitude of nations:

▶ No longer shall your name be called Abram, but your name shall be Abraham, for I have made you the father of a multitude of nations.
Genesis 17: 5

Names are included in powerful messages from our Lord: Note: a vesture is a robe.

▶ 12, His eyes were as a flame of fire, and on his head were many crowns; and he had a name written, that no man knew, but he himself.

13, And he was clothed with a vesture dipped in blood: and his name is called The Word of God.

Revelation 19:12-13

And, we receive the most blessed, powerful promise from the Higher Power, the Creator God, the Holy One, the Redeemer of a "name" of God and New Jerusalem being written upon us:

▶ Him that overcometh will I make a pillar in the temple of my God, and he shall go no more out: and I will write upon him the name of my God, and the name of the city of my God, which is new Jerusalem, which cometh down out of heaven from my God: and I will write upon him my new name.

Revelation 3:12

There appears an aspect of "Name" that is not explained. There is a reason that the name is being written, and an effect because it is being written by God.

The Lord writing a Name on someone would have an effect on that person. What would that effect be upon the individual that has the new name of God written on him? I would expect that effect to be spectacularly awesome.

Not every point is knowable. Aspects of "name" are not fully revealed to us - as not everything is fully revealed. The Disciples asked Jesus specifically about the end of times He replied:

▶ But of that day and hour knoweth no man, no, not the angels of heaven, but my Father only.

Matthew 24:36

Also Daniel was told to "shut up the words, and seal the book":

▶ 1. And at that time shall Michael stand up, the great prince which standeth for the children of thy people: and there shall be a time of trouble, such as never was since there was a nation even to that same time: and at that time thy people shall be delivered, every one that shall be found written in the book.

2. And many of them that sleep in the dust of the earth shall awake, some to everlasting life, and some to shame and everlasting contempt.

3. And they that be wise shall shine as the brightness of the firmament; and they that turn many to righteousness as the stars forever and ever.

4. But thou, O Daniel, shut up the words, and seal the book, even to the time of the end: many shall run to and fro, and knowledge shall be increased.

Daniel 12: 1-4

When the Apostles, Peter and John were confronted by a begging man who was lame since birth, Peter answered with a gift in "the name of Jesus Christ of Nazareth:"

▶ Then Peter said, Silver and gold have I none; but such as I have give I thee: In the name of Jesus Christ of Nazareth rise up and walk.

Acts 3:6

So then what is in a name? A name represents oneself. A name summarizes oneself. A name carries memories. A name identifies oneself with his family. A name represents or is relationships. A name is the way one sees oneself or oneself is expressed. A name reveals Himself in knowledge, knowing the Lord.

Calling upon a name evokes and or directs. Therefore the calling of a name or naming of one connects the named with the one named. Calling upon the name of the Lord is powerful. Whereas naming a child after mortals or angels connects to the memories, creates relationships and may have significant impact on the child's forming and development.

In Genesis, Adam named the animals and then after the Lord created "Woman" the Lord brought her unto the man:

▶ And Adam said, This is now bone of my bones, and flesh of my flesh: she shall be called Woman, because she was taken out of Man.

Genesis 2: 23

It is interesting that it was not until after the serpent's deception, after the "eating of the apple," and after the Lord confronted the three of them in the garden and the Lord had pronounced their punishment that then Adam names Eve:

▶ And Adam called his wife's name Eve: because she was the mother of all living.

Genesis 3:20

And, regarding "name" another incredibly awesome promise of "an everlasting name that shall not be cut off" by our blessed, protector, Higher Power, the Creator God, the Holy One, the Redeemer:

▶ 4. For thus saith the Lord unto the eunuchs that keep my Sabbaths, and choose the things that please me, and take hold of my covenant;

5. Even unto them will I give in mine house and within my walls a place and a name better than of sons and of daughters: I will give them an everlasting name, that shall not be cut off.

6. Also the sons of the stranger, that join themselves to the Lord, to serve him, and to love the name of the Lord, to be his servants, every one that keepeth the Sabbath from polluting it, and taketh hold of my covenant;

Isaiah 56: 4-6

If you have not considered names from this perspective you may want to review your nicknames or personalized names that you call your loved ones. For example there is a difference in calling a man "Billy" or calling him "William." Cleary there are different connotations in play.

Even changing a name slightly would carry that changing effect through the connections of the memories, recollections or other connections of the named after relatives, angels or family/ancestor relationships back to the person who had his/her name changed. Recall, Abraham's name was only changed from Abram.

And, apparently there is a lot more implications from the meaning in names than just being a popular name or that the name has a nice sound to it, which is also important and can be very good.

▶ A good name is rather to be chosen than great riches, and loving favour rather than silver and gold.

Proverbs 22:1

Jesus Christ is our Savior. Call upon the name of the Lord, the Lord of Abraham, Isaac and Jacob. He hears us. Ask and you will receive. Get right with the Lord. He knows your heart. Delight and commit one's way to the Lord. Obey His Commandments. Do not Complain.

Thank Lord Jesus, Praise Father, Son and Holy Ghost. Hold in your heart the good things, things that are true, honest, just, pure, and lovely.

You are saved by the sacrifice of Jesus on the cross. You cannot earn salvation through your own works. God has raised Jesus from the dead. Jesus loves you while you are yet a sinner.

Keep the faith. All things are possible by the Higher Power. Tune-In Heaven and receive the blessings, the protection of God Almighty, the Protector and enter into the Joy of the Lord, the Higher Power, the Creator God, the Holy One, the Redeemer.

In Jesus name we pray.

Amen